IT HURTS SO BAD, LORD!

Andrew D. Lester

BROADMAN PRESS
Nashville, Tennessee

© Copyright 1976 • Broadman Press
All rights reserved.

4252-38
ISBN: 0-8054-5238-9

Dewey Decimal Classification: 242.4
Subject headings: CONSOLATION//CHRISTIAN LIFE

Library of Congress Catalog Card Number: 75-42860
Printed in the United States of America

To
Andrew and Dorothy Lester,
my father and mother

Who provided loving support during the many crises which occurred in the process of raising six children.

Who taught us that crises should not have the last word because, "We know that in everything God works for good with those who love him" (Rom. 8:28).

Who communicate in numerous ways their faith that

"neither death, nor life, nor angels, nor principalities, nor things present, nor things to come, nor powers, nor height, nor depth, nor anything else in all creation, will be able to separate us from the love of God in Christ Jesus our Lord (Rom. 8:38-39).

CONTENTS

Preface

From the critical moment of birth through the process of dying, each human being must come face to face with many crises. These crises have various meanings to each individual, and each of us responds to them in a variety of ways. We can be defeated by crises or we can be "more than conquerors through him who loved us" (Rom. 8:37).

This book deals with some of the most common and difficult crises. It is my hope that you, the reader, will learn through this book that you are not alone in experiencing your particular crisis. Your experiences are shared among a multitude of other persons. I also hope that the resources of your Christian faith can become more available and meaningful to you as you read.

I am grateful to those many people who have been my teachers by sharing with me their personal struggles. They have allowed me to participate in their pilgrimages through the various crises discussed in this book. Some were patients in hospitals, some were counselees, and still others were students or colleagues at Southeastern Baptist Theological Seminary, Wake Forest University, or the School of Pastoral Care. Their experiences are the heart of this book and reflected in every sentence.

Many of these people read selected chapters and gave helpful feedback. Several persons, including Dr. Fred Horton, Dr. Ted Dougherty, Dr. Mahan Siler, Rev. George Bowman, and Mrs. Freddie Lou Haworth, read many of the chapters and gave helpful counsel as the book took shape.

I am also grateful for the Baptist State Convention of North Carolina, the North Carolina Baptist Hospital, and John E. Lynch, the Chief Executive Officer, for providing me with an exciting context in which to share ministries of teaching, counseling, and crisis intervention.

My secretary (translate "right arm"), Miss Jean Aiken, typed innumerable drafts of each chapter and gave of her considerable talent in preparing the manuscript. My children, Scott and Denise, gave some of their "time with Daddy" to this book with more understanding than I thought possible at ages seven and three. Scott provided two types of inspiration when his prayer at the table changed over several months from, "God, please help Daddy write a good book," to "God, please help Daddy hurry up and finish the book!" Judy, my wife, was her usual steadfast self, helping me in varied ways to complete the task. Writing the book would have been a more difficult crisis without her understanding and supportive love.

1
When It Seems Hopeless
(The Crisis of Depression)

Why consider depression a crisis? Depression, unless it is severe, does not affect our lives in quite the same way as the other crises discussed in this book. It is not usually the same life-shaking trauma, nor does it produce the same intense emotional upheaval as grief, dying, or divorce.

I consider depression a crisis, however, because when we are depressed it disrupts our lives and the lives of those with whom we are related. Depression robs life of happiness, excitement, and joy. It is difficult to experience meaningful relationships and either give or receive love when despondent. We get moody, refuse to talk, withdraw from those we love, dislike ourselves, and are characterized by sadness, apathy, and self-reproach. When depressed we do not function well in our jobs or take pleasure in our other responsibilities. Despondency usually leads to a despairing feeling about our religious life. It affects our perceptions and experiences of God and our expressions of faith. For these reasons, I consider depression a crisis.

While some of the more earthshaking crises, like death and divorce, happen relatively few times to one individual, depression can occur frequently. It produces a series of minicrises in our lives and in the lives of those with whom we relate. If episodes of despondency and despair occur frequently, the cumulative effect can have the same impact as one of the more intense traumas.

Depression is also included in this book because most people are affected by it in some way. Many of us experience mild depressive moods which we call "the blues," "feeling low," or "being down." Other people feel themselves to be sad, lonely, empty, unhappy, and dejected, when they are really describing a time of depression. In its severe stages, of course, depression is even more of a crisis. Beck says, "Depression is the most common psychiatric disorder treated in office practice and out-patient clinics," and points to authorities who estimate that 12 percent of the adult population experience episodes of depression severe enough to warrant some type of medical treatment.[1]

Many readers will have experienced some deeper depressions. You may be taking some medication or seeing a psychiatrist or counselor for help with depression. Others of you will have been depressed but were unwilling to seek help or perhaps not have realized what you were experiencing. Still others deal with less intense periods of despondency which are not acute but which interfere with living. These periods of time are frustrating, annoying, and disruptive. Finding out the cause of depression can enable us to deal more effectively with it and claim more of the "abundant life" that God wills for us.

Recognizing Depression

We will describe the way depression affects people in order to help you clearly identify when you are dealing with this particular emotional problem. Depression makes itself known through physical, mental, emotional, spiritual, and behavioral symptoms.

Physical Effects of Depression

Depression makes itself known through its multiple effects on our body and its behavior. It affects how our bodies feel to us, how we feel toward our bodies, and how we function physically.[2]

Depression, for example, affects our respiratory system. It seems difficult to breathe and there seems to be a tightening of the chest ("I feel like a rope is tied tightly around my chest." "I feel like something is squeezing my chest so that I can't breathe"). This results in feeling "short of breath." You will find yourself "sighing" as if every so often you must forcibly draw air into your lungs.

Eating patterns are disturbed by depression. You may have a sluggish appetite, eat very little (and that only because you feel you have to exist), and be losing weight. Some people, however, begin to stay hungry all the time, eat compulsively (even when not hungry), and gain weight. Many overweight people suffer from a low-level of chronic depression.

Sleeping patterns are also disrupted. Some people fall asleep easily but awaken early in the morning unable to get back to sleep. Others cannot get to sleep before one or two o'clock in the morning but then sleep heavily and are hard to arouse. Still others sleep fitfully, waking and sleeping at intervals during the whole night. Instead of awakening refreshed in the morning, despondent people usually feel just as tired as the night before.

The "blues" retard our energy levels. It is difficult to do anything which demands physical action. It seems that things we pick up are heavier than usual, and climbing steps seems to be exhausting work. Physical actions like mowing the grass, sweeping the basement, scrubbing the floor, or playing sports seem like an impossible task. Just getting out of bed, up from a chair, or away from the table seems laborious. A general sense of fatigue and chronic tiredness grips us during depression. You have no "pep." Your "get up and go" has gone. Little reserve strength is available. When you are despondent, sexual interests are diminished, and the stimuli which may have aroused you under other circumstances do not seem at all erotic.

When "down" you probably do not take care of your body and its appearance in the usual fashion. Because our energy levels and motivation are so low, it is difficult to bathe, wash and comb hair, shave, or dress neatly. Some people wear their older, drabber clothes when dejected.

Crying spells come often for some depressed people. You may experience intense, agitated crying for which there seems no cause. Others experience periods of more subdued tearfulness and weeping. Still others do not cry but wish they could. ("If I could only cry,

I know I would feel better," I often hear people say.)

Mental Reactions

Depression not only affects our physical functioning but also our mental reactions and our thinking patterns. In depressive moods, for example, your memory may be poor and you may forget things you are supposed to remember. You may find that your ability to concentrate is impaired. The lack of energy affects our ability to think clearly, and our feeling of hopelessness makes us doubt that any good will result from thinking.

Many find it difficult to make decisions when depressed. Others, however, make panic decisions, because of their depression, which are neither appropriate nor responsible. This relates to the fact that when depressed we may not be in good contact with reality, lack orientation to what is happening around us, and make mistakes of judgment. These are some ways in which depression affects our ability to think and reason.

Emotional Dynamics

Depression is often characterized by a chronic feeling of anxiety, which may be subdued but is usually present in some degree. This anxiety has many causes and is both a contributor to and the result of our concern over the depression and its effect on us. Sometimes this anxiety becomes intense and can reach panic proportions. The source of our anxiety is often unknown. We may have only vague concerns about the future, or "what might happen," or of being alone. At times, this anxiety focuses on more specific worries. For example: "I am going to lose my mind." "Something is going to happen to a member of my family." "I have lost my faith." At other times the causes of anxiety are known or can be known through self-awareness. These causes include some of the things discussed later under "causes." These anxieties and fears contribute to some of the following emotional responses.

Hopelessness. One of the most obvious emotional experiences of depression is the attitude of hopelessness/helplessness. When "down," it is difficult to feel that any hope is present in the situation or that any help can be forthcoming. When despondent, we are usually gloomy and pessimistic ("I've tried everything." "Nothing can help now." "I'm at the end of my rope."). We feel "boxed in" or "trapped" and perceive that things will at best stay the same and probably get worse. You may feel that the future is black and that none of the problems can be solved. You may also experience how difficult it is to take any action because of the assumption, "It won't do any good."

Worthlessness. Another common component of emotional despair is the feeling of worthlessness. "It's all my fault," expresses the cry of those who accept a great deal of blame for something that is taking place in their lives. "If it weren't for me . . ." indicates the feeling of those who feel responsible for some event or happening. Feelings of inadequacy and ineptitude are also expressed in words such as, "I caused it," or, "I'm a failure." This feeling of worthlessness affects our perceptions of life's basic meanings. "Life isn't worthwhile any longer" or "I don't know why I should go on living" expresses the feeling of those whose sense of worthlessness pervades their entire existence. Needless to say, when this feeling of worthlessness combines with a sense of hopelessness, suicide can seem to be the only alternative.

Apathy. Boredom and apathy are also characteristic of depressive moods. Things and people that were once important parts of your life are now related to with disinterest. Your job is not stimulating, family activities are a drag, church affairs are not exciting, and hobbies are no longer fun. You pay no attention to your favorite TV program, your favorite team, or to the increasing messiness of your house. It is hard to respond to any of the regular stimuli like conversation, affection, and challenge.

Physical complaints. The combination of real physical symptoms and the negative, self-blaming emotional state make the depressed person feel ill. You may find yourself complaining about your physical problems more often when you are depressed. We feel so lousy that it is easy to consider ourselves as sick. It is also true that family, friends, and employers are more accepting and understanding of us when we are sick than when we are depressed. Therefore, it is easier to complain about our ills and fit into a "sick-role" than to claim we are depressed. The sick role helps us avoid the fact that we are dealing with an emotional problem by allowing us to consider that we have a physical problem.

Spiritual Symptoms

The emotional and mental reactions that are present in the experience of depression surface in an individual's religious life. For example, one reason we move into the sick role, instead of facing the fact that we are depressed, is because of the guilt we feel over the "laziness" which results from our low-energy level, lack of motivation, and apathy. The feelings of boredom and apathy often affect religious life. Our participation in church may slacken or terminate, and our personal religious experiences do not seem to have the same meaning to us. This can create strong feelings of guilt and the fear that God will rebuke us or cut himself off from us.

The hopeless/helpless mood may create feelings of distance from God. ("I feel so far away from God." "My prayers go no higher than the ceiling.") We get the feeling that even God could not help. ("God can't make it clear to me what I should do." "The Spirit has left me.")

The worthless theme running through our despondency also affects our religious thoughts. The feeling of failure may lead you to feel that God is dissatisfied. Feelings of blame and responsibility lead some to believe that God is angry with them and is out to get them. The emotional pain of depression can be perceived as God's punishment.

The worthless feelings lead one to experience alienation from God. I remember, when doing a unit of clinical training at a mental hospital, the number of patients who thought they had somehow committed the unpardonable sin or "grieved the Spirit," despite the fact that they were often unable to describe these sins.

This sense of sin, which is so predominant for the depressed

Christian, is complicated by the feeling that their guilt can never be removed. The hopeless/helpless attitude, plus the feelings of worthlessness, make it difficult to imagine that forgiveness could ever be forthcoming. When despondent we feel that mercy is unobtainable and God's acceptance a lie.

Another symptom of depression in the Christian may be the questioning of salvation. Many evangelical Christians who get depressed ask the question, "Am I saved?" They worry that those who have real faith would not experience the kind of depression that they are experiencing. Therefore, they think something has happened to their faith. The strong feelings of sinfulness and guilt make them question their right to be a "child of God."

Changes in Behavior

Despondency is not only felt in the body and experienced in the emotional realm, but it also affects our behavior and our functioning.

One of the most common behavioral responses to depression is withdrawal and isolation. When despondent we are not usually interested in the company of others; in fact, interpersonal relating seems difficult to the point of embarrassment. The physical symptoms are easily used as buffers. ("I don't feel well tonight." "I'm going to bed early." "I can't come, I've lost too much sleep.") The "blues" keep us from enjoying conversation; and, of course, we do not feel worthy of anybody's attention.

The feeling of worthlessness can lead to irresponsible behavior on the part of the depressed individual. Since family and friends are trying to be assuring and supportive, they keep communicating that the depressed individual is good, worthy, and well liked. The depressed person may have to act in some unusual way to convince them of his or her worthlessness. Alcoholic binges, sexual escapades, buying sprees, or shoplifting may be the despondent person's way of saying, "I told you I'm rotten to the core." Any unusual negative behavior may indicate depression.

Despondency can also spark "panic decisions" which can lead to trouble. I remember one counselee who became acutely depressed and tried to sell his private business. He and his wife had worked hard for fifteen years to build the business, but suddenly he was willing to sell it at a loss to the first buyer. Luckily his wife realized this was illogical. She was able to hospitalize him for treatment of depression. I have known other people who have chosen to get pregnant, separate, get married, quit a job, drop out of school, or make some other decision which was unwise for that time and place. The decisions were made out of desperation and in hopes that it would ease their plight. As hopelessness sets in, further decisions and changes might be attempted to alleviate the situation and bring resolution, each being less helpful than the previous.

The boredom and apathy feeling often shows itself in a "drifting" pattern of behavior. Lacking interest in anything and not caring what happens, a despondent person may just float along through life with no zest, no excitement, and no joy. This is particularly true of chronic depression. Young people may actually drift geographically, moving from place to place and group to group in a noncommitted way. They have no purposes in life to strive for, no goals to aim at, no causes to fight for, no future for which to plan.

Depression may express itself in what has been called a manic phase, characterized by the opposite of many things already mentioned. Instead of depleted energy there may be a surplus, so that the individual is "charged up" or "high." Rather than indifference and withdrawal, the manic phase is characterized by overextension and involvement. Instead of having no goals and purposes, the manic person will have unrealistic goals and objectives. Individuals in the manic stage may begin working two shifts, take on extra committee work, volunteer for many projects, and in general act as if there is not a moment to spare.

Causes of Depression

No unanimous decision has been reached by psychiatrists and other behavioral scientists about the cause of depression. Some clinicians and investigators think that depression is always caused by organic factors: that is, chemical imbalances in the body, hormonal changes, or diseases and infections of the brain and central nervous system. Other investigators believe depression is always caused by psychological factors such as guilt, anger, grief, or maladaptive thinking patterns. Some theorists believe depression is caused by some combination of organic and psychological factors, while others feel some kinds of depression are caused by organic factors and other kinds of depression by psychological factors.

Philosophers, theologians, and some behavioral scientists also think that depression is affected by spiritual/existential factors. They usually describe this depressive life-experience with the word despair.

It is not within our interests here to describe possible biological factors in depression. Even if I did describe them, you would not be able to discover whether or not they affected your depressiveness without consulting a physician/psychiatrist. We will describe some of the psychological factors which often underlie depression.

Anger

Students of human behavior believe anger is a significant contributing factor to depression.[3] We will define anger as our hostile response to situations or relationships in which we feel hurt, attacked, threatened, or treated unjustly. In our society, expression of anger, along with other forms of aggression, is often discouraged. Many people grow up in homes where the expression of negative feelings is not allowed. Schools do not make much room for angry behavior. The Christian church has often communicated that to feel anger, much less express it, means a person is not being Christlike. Many individuals, therefore, grow up thinking and feeling that their Christian faith and anger are mutually exclusive, that being angry is sinful.

It is no wonder, therefore, that many people are not able to express the negative feelings generated within them while existing in this real world. When they have been manipulated, used, hurt, disappointed, frustrated, rejected, or cheated, they suppress their angry response. They run from conflict and do not allow arguments, disagreements, or other negative interaction to take place between them and parents, spouses, children, or colleagues. Angry feelings are censored, held back, and pushed down inside one's own self. Later these angry feelings become directed at the self (called introjection by psychologists) as if the self were the villain. This anger aimed at the self surfaces as self-blame, self-criticism, and feelings of worthlessness, all of which can lead to depression. Anger at the self can be so intense that it leads to suicide. ("I am so bad it would be better for them if I were dead.")

I am an example of how unrecognized and unexpressed anger can create periods of despondency. Anger was rarely expressed in my home. As a young boy, I had one threatening experience with the anger of a relative which convinced me that anger was dangerous. Later as a teenager, I got in a fight and was frightened by the extent of my anger when fully expressed. I decided again that anger was dangerous. I also began to believe, as my Christian identity crystallized, that anger was unchristlike. I suppressed my anger, therefore, never expressing hostile feelings and even reaching the point where I did not recognize these feelings when they occurred.

In my early and middle twenties, I experienced depressive moods characterized by apathy and the inability to motivate myself to get things done. I did not understand the source of this depressiveness. I was finally helped, however, to see how this unrecognized anger was using up my energies and sabotaging my will power. With this understanding, I learned to recognize anger in myself when it occurred and handle it more responsibly. (See the following chapter.) Then depressive moods became much less of a problem.

Guilt

Another major dynamic in despondency is guilt which results from two different, but overlapping, personal experiences. Guilt is a response of some individuals to their feelings of inferiority and inadequacy which generate within them a sense of shame and worthlessness. These individuals appear to feel guilty for just being alive and usually make few demands of other people.

Guilt can also be the response of individuals to thoughts or actions in their lives which they consider sinful. Guilt is pervasive in our culture and affects many people in many ways, one of which is depression. What lies beneath this guilt?

The depressed person usually has what psychoanalysts call a strong "superego." The superego has two parts: (1) the conscience, which is our sense of right and wrong, and (2) the ideal self, which is the image we have of the ideal person we think we can be or should be.[4] This internalized belief about what we should do (conscience) or what we should be (self-ideal) is developed in our early relationships with parents, other significant people (friends and relatives), and institutions (school and church).

When our conscience is violated, when we feel that we have transgressed our basic value system, the result is guilt. When this guilt is not resolved through awareness, confession, acceptance of forgiveness, and perhaps restitution, we feel bad about ourselves. We worry about what other people think of us and feel that we have been unfaithful to our Christian commitments. Depression will often occur. Sometimes the depressed person is not aware of thinking or acting in a way he or she considers sinful and, therefore, is not consciously aware of feeling guilty. At other times an individual is aware but is so caught up in the cycle of feeling worthless and blaming himself that he or she does not perceive forgiveness is deserved or even possible. Hopelessness and worthlessness are strong factors in the resulting depression.

When we fall short of our ideal self, we experience shame—the feeling that we are totally inadequate, incapable, undeserving. We develop low self-esteem, disbelieving that we are worth anything to anybody and wondering why God let us live. Depression can result, with strong feelings of self-blame and worthlessness.

To speak personally, again, every time I experienced anger from my late teens through my middle twenties, I experienced guilt, for both reasons mentioned above. First, I felt that I had sinned by transgressing an ethical code I had set for myself, "Do not be angry." Secondly, I fell short of my ideal self by failing to live up to an expectation I had established for my own Christian life, which was to experience no anger. Needless to say, this guilt compounded my experience of depression. It was not until I learned more about the Christian faith and anger that I could think differently.

Western culture teaches strongly that every individual is responsible for himself or herself. When anything goes wrong, it is natural to assume that it is one's own fault. When a person loses a job, hears that his adolescent son got into trouble, or finds out that a friend does not like him or her anymore, it is easy to assume at both conscious and unconscious levels that we are to blame. This can result in a chronic feeling of guilt and responsibility for all the negative things which occur in our lives.

Grief

When we experience the loss of something which has been of significance, the result is grief. Our identities and meanings in life can be heavily dependent on our environment, particularly the people who inhabit it. When a meaningful part of our environment is lost, or we are separated from a significant person, we suffer a psychological wound. As described in the chapter on grief, the anxiety created by this loss or separation can shake the foundations of meaning in our lives, call our faith into question, disturb our perceptions of life, make us feel both anger and guilt, and bring on many self-doubts and self-criticisms. Needless to say, any or all of these can lead to depression.

Grief can be expressed over all kinds of losses. Perhaps the heaviest loss comes when death claims someone close to us. Grief is also experienced over physical losses, such as losing a part or function of the body or losing one's health because of a debilitating disease or accident. Aging carries with it the potential loss of sexual capabilities, diminishing senses (particularly seeing and hearing), and the loss of usefulness (which in our society is a value and a commodity). Still other grief results from social losses such as broken courtships, separation and divorce, moving to a new place, and losing a job. Sometimes an event which brings loss of prestige can also produce grief.

As we have described in the chapter on grief, one of the normal ingredients of bereavement is the experience of depression. Despondency over a bereavement is usually transitory and will lift as the grief process continues. If for whatever reasons the grief process is thwarted, however, then the depression can deepen and lengthen to the point where help is needed to break its chain. You might be able to trace your depression to a specific loss, or series of losses, which you have suffered.

Responding to Depression

If you are wrestling with depression, you should consider making an appointment with your doctor for a thorough medical checkup. Since physiological factors are present in depression, it is important to have a physician evaluate your overall health to find whether any physical problem is a contributing factor. You will share, I hope, with him or her the whole range of symptoms you are experiencing, including the mental and emotional ones. If your personal physician does not feel comfortable in treating depression, he probably will refer you to one who does. If you do not have a family physician or do not feel free to discuss these symptoms with him or her, then ask someone you trust, like your pastor, to refer you to a physician who has experience with and feels comfortable with depression.

Medications have been developed which can be very helpful in combating the chemical changes which depression has caused in your body. Sometimes, of course, it might be the chemical changes which have brought about the depression. Medication can be significant in helping you function adequately and normally even when the root causes of the depression have not been discovered.

When the basic causes of your depression are psychological in origin, that is in experiences, perceptions, and feelings you have had in the past, then seeing a psychotherapist or other trained counselor can be extremely helpful. Talking over your personal pilgrimage with an objective but interested and knowledgeable professional can help you gain insight into your experience of depression. You may gain understanding of an unresolved grief experience from long ago. Or you might come to grips with long suppressed amounts of anger generated in your life by specific persons or events, but which have not been handled directly. Or you may find out that you have suffered from low self-esteem and a feeling of shame about your existence. Or, again, you might find out that heavy burdens of guilt have generated your despair.

Many pastors are trained to talk with people about their emotional and spiritual concerns. Since you might feel that your problems are more easily shared with a pastor than with a psychotherapist, I hope you will search out a minister who is trained and enter into conversations with him or her. They can help you understand the relationship of your depression to the emotional and spiritual concerns we discuss in the next chapter.

When depressed, it is hard for us to take initiative in receiving help. Some friend or family member with whom you can share these burdens may be willing to make appointments for you. It is not always comfortable for family and friends to be around you when depressed, and some of your relationships may have been negatively affected. Since a feeling of community and love is so important in overcoming depression, I hope you will take steps to reestablish these relationships.

The Christian faith includes a message about our struggles with anger, guilt, and grief, which may be helpful to you in overcoming depression. You will also want to explore some of the spiritual dimensions of depression and despair. Both of these concerns are discussed in the following chapter.

Notes

1. Aaron T. Beck, *The Diagnosis and Management of Depression* (Philadelphia: University of Pennsylvania Press, 1973), p. vii.

2. See Beck, pp. 9-40; also Leonard Cammer, *Up From Depression* (New York: Simon & Schuster, Inc., 1969).

3. See Willard Gaylin, *The Meaning of Despair: Psychoanalytic Contributions to the Understanding of Depression* (New York: Science House, Inc., 1968).

4. Frederic F. Flach, *The Secret Strength of Depression* (New York: J. B. Lippincott Co., 1974), pp. 164-165.

2
Where Are You, Lord?
(The Recovery of Hope)

If you have experienced depression, you know firsthand the hopelessness, despondency, sadness, and apathy which we described in the previous chapter. You have tasted life when it had no joy and excitement and when nothing seemed to be worthwhile or meaningful. For us as Christians, depression impairs and inhibits our spiritual existence. We feel with the psalmist who said, "My soul is cast down within me" (42:6). We understand his question to God, "Why hast thou forgotten me?" (v. 9).

You may think, in fact, that to be despondent is to lack faith. You may believe, therefore, that you have forfeited the right to draw on your Christian faith as a resource for dealing with depression and despair. But being depressed does not necessarily mean that you possess no faith. Actually, many persons of faith have experienced depression and despair. Moses (Num. 11:15), Elijah (1 Kings 19:4), Job (Job 10:1), and Jeremiah (Jer. 8:18-21) were among the biblical heroes who experienced dejection and despondency.

It is not always clear when depression affects our spiritual existence and when our spiritual questions and problems cause despair. We do know that they often go hand-in-hand. When a person becomes depressed, it affects his or her spiritual life. When a person's spiritual center is under attack or threatened, despair can be the result. In this chapter, we shall discuss what the Christian faith says about three major psychological causes of depression and then discuss some of the spiritual problems which either cause despair or grow out of depression.

A Christian Response to Anger, Guilt, and Grief

In the last chapter, we discussed three psychological factors which can contribute to the experience of depression. To recover hope, to reclaim joy, to escape the quicksand of despair, we must have the courage to overcome anger, guilt, and grief, when any or all of them are at the root of the problem. Our Christian faith does provide resources for understanding and challenging the hold on our life which anger, guilt, and grief may hold.

The Christian and Anger

In the previous chapter we described the power of anger, when kept within oneself and aimed at the self, to cause depression. We briefly described our culture's discouragement of healthy expression of anger and noted that the Christian church is particularly guilty for communicating that anger in any shape or form is sinful. I believe this to be a false teaching and a misrepresentation of the gospel. Many Christians do themselves harm by thinking that it is unchristian either to feel or express anger.

What is a Christian view of anger? First of all, to feel anger is a common, normal, human experience. When our "personhood," our ego, is threatened, one of the possible human responses is to become hostile. What should humans do when they feel these negative feelings? Some would have us believe that we should pay them no attention, suppress them, and swallow the adrenaline which is stirred within us in order to be more Christlike. To do this, however, is to deny part of our human nature. It also assumes that Jesus did not experience anger and that the New Testament always views anger as a negative. This leads to a second point.

Did Jesus himself experience anger? Mark records an interaction between Jesus and the Pharisees over the question of healing a man on the sabbath. When Jesus realized that they were waiting to accuse him of breaking the sabbath laws, "he looked around at them with anger, grieved at their hardness of heart" (3:5). Jesus must have been feeling some negative feelings when he made a whip and drove the money changers out of the Temple and turned over their tables

(John 2:13-16). These actions and words reminded the disciples of the psalm which said, "Zeal for thy house will consume me" (Ps. 69:9; John 2:17). Most Christians believe that Jesus was sinless; so if he were angry, it follows that anger is not necessarily evil or sinful.

We must also listen to the Pauline message to the members of the church at Ephesus. In the fourth chapter, the writer is challenging these Christians to reach "mature manhood" (v. 13), "to grow up" into Christ (v. 15), and to "be renewed in the spirit of your minds" (v. 23). He suggests one way this can be accomplished:

Therefore, putting away falsehood, let every one speak the truth with his neighbor, for we are members one of another. Be angry but do not sin; do not let the sun go down on your anger, and give no opportunity to the devil (Eph. 4:25-27).

When angry it is necessary to deal with the anger in truth and in love (Eph. 4:15). Since we are "members one of another" we must relate openly and honestly and that means facing the hostilities which are present within us. However, we cannot let this anger be destructive. If we "let the sun go down" before our anger is expressed and resolved, then it can begin to poison our system and give opportunity for sin. One way it can poison us is to create depression. Unresolved anger can grow into hate, which leads to estrangement and alienation, which can progress into despair.

All this is to say that when you feel anger within you, it does not mean that you have sinned. It does mean that the possibility for sin is present. That can happen if the anger goes unrecognized or unresolved and becomes an infection in our relationships or becomes destructive and hurtful to other people. Our responsibility, therefore, is to handle our anger in appropriate, responsible ways which are compatible with love rather than selfishness and hate.

The first step in handling anger responsibly is awareness. We must "tune in" our innermost thoughts and feelings so that we can recognize and name any negative feeling which arises. As soon as we recognize and name it, we have the possibility of handling it creatively. When negative feelings go unrecognized, they cause trouble by "leaking out" in ways of which we are not aware. For example, I know that I allow unrecognized anger to leak out in sarcastic humor. I also know that when I experience anger, but am unaware of it, I am more harsh with my children than they deserve.

After awareness comes identification of the source of the negative feeling. Why am I angry? Who or what made me angry? Was I treated unjustly? Do I feel as though I have fallen short of some goal? Our negative feelings grow from some "soil," some interaction with another person, some unmet personal need, or some event or situation. Our anger is usually aimed at something or someone. What is the target? Identifying the source is important and makes the next step possible.

After identification of the source we can decide on the appropriateness or inappropriateness of our anger. We have a moral obligation under God to evaluate the validity of our anger, to decide whether or not it is ethical or unethical.

What criteria can a Christian use to decide? It is not a simple question to answer, but I think the solution must be in our concept of love. We have a responsibility to love God, to love our neighbor, and to love our self. Anger is ethical when it is an expression of our love in any of these three areas. For example, Jesus' anger when he went into the Temple to drive out the money changers was certainly related to his love for God and his protest against unrighteousness. His anger at the Pharisees while healing the man with a withered hand must have been related to his love for that man and his anger that the Pharisees would rather have the man crippled than to break a man-made law concerning the sabbath. God has loved us enough to be angry at injustice between humans. We must also be willing to love enough to feel angry when injustice takes place between people. In fact, God historically has challenged his people through the prophets to stand up against injustice.

If we are to love ourselves appropriately, and affirm ourselves as children of God, then we may be appropriately angry when someone is treating us unjustly, manipulating us, hurting us in some way, or treating us unfairly. Certainly it is important to turn the other cheek (Matt. 5:39), forgive seventy times seven (Matt. 18:22), and be slow to anger (Prov. 15:18). But turning the other cheek, forgiving, and being careful not to let our anger kindle too quickly, is not the same as pretending that the actions of another person did not make us angry. Rather, these responses are several of the responsible and appropriate ways in which a Christian can handle his or her anger. Getting out of the way, reporting to the police, divorcing, and spanking are other ways that may be appropriate.

When anger is childish, immature, petty, or jealous, it is unjustified. When anger grows out of our selfishness it is a different problem.

After deciding about the ethical validity of our anger, we may take the next step of deciding how to handle it responsibly. If the anger is valid and is a loving response, then the responsibility is ours to direct this anger towards the appropriate threat. We may need to take some action, express our feelings toward particular people, create a confrontation. However, if the anger is selfish and a manifestation of our own immaturity and inadequacy, then our response should be to express our anger toward ourselves with some understanding person and to take steps toward self-understanding and personal growth. We may need to take action to correct some interaction with another person or to apologize for some thought or deed.

If anger is handled in these ways, we shall do much to spare ourselves from depression.

The Christian and Guilt

We mentioned earlier that unresolved guilt was a causal factor in depression. We indicated that this guilt was related to two somewhat different experiences. One of these experiences of guilt grows from our reaction to feelings of inadequacy and inferiority which we call shame. The second experience of guilt grows from our reaction to thoughts and actions which we believe are sinful because they contradict our ethical and moral ideals.

With reference to the shame which you might experience, the

Christian gospel proclaims God's acceptance of our humanity. After God had created man, he said that his creation "was very good" (Gen. 1:31). He created us to have fellowship with him. We are created in God's image and are the crown of his creation! You are special to God, one of his children, a person for whom his love is so strong that nothing can separate you from it (Rom. 8:37-39).

But if you are depressed, it is hard for you to believe this. You feel as though you have failed him in some way. You do not feel as though your talents and gifts are worth anything. You are like the little drummer boy who was caught without a present and do not feel that just your self is worth anything. Perhaps you are feeling like a failure because of some specific event: you think you failed as a parent, you lost your job, or your marriage broke up. The Christian gospel, however, proclaims that God accepts our finitude, our failures, our shortcomings. His grace is still shared with us and his love still flows toward us!

With reference to specific words or deeds which you believe transgressed ethical and moral values, the Christian faith proclaims forgiveness. Who among us does not think and act in unloving ways? Who among us can claim no sin? Yes, we are guilty and have fallen short of God's will for our relationship to him, to other people, and to ourselves. Our response to this can be to choose despair and self-reproach, wallowing in our guilt and condemnation. Or, we can confess our sins, knowing that God "is faithful and just, and will forgive our sins and cleanse us from all unrighteousness" (1 John 1:9).

Carrying guilt around in the closets of our mind and the back pockets of our hearts can surely be a depressing existence. Let us remind ourselves anew that the God of love makes forgiveness possible!

The Christian and Grief

We have also said that unresolved grief over significant losses and separations can lead to depression. We will not speak to this concern here because in other chapters we have described at length the experience of grief and the healing which is necessary for returning to an abundant life.

Spiritual Problems in Despair

We have described three of the major psychological factors in depression and also suggested a Christian response. Down through the ages, however, persons of faith have described the spiritual dimensions of existence which can lead to despair. It should be added that any of the psychological factors already described can be an outgrowth of these spiritual dimensions of despair. We will describe three of these spiritual problems and suggest how the Christian gospel speaks to them through faith, hope, and love. These dimensions are often interwoven within despair and feed on each other.

Emptiness and Meaninglessness

Paul Tillich has written about man's anxiety over meaninglessness.[1] He begins with the assumption that humans have a spiritual life which they take seriously. He calls this having "ultimate concern" about our "spiritual center." It is this spiritual center which gives a basic meaning to all of our life. Tillich says that it provides an answer to the questions we ask about the meaning of existence. Needless to say, when something happens to our ultimate concern, when we are cut off from our spiritual center, then we are overcome by, and plunged into, despair.

To overcome meaninglessness the Christian must have the courage to exercise faith even in the face of this meaninglessness. We must have faith in our experiences with God, even though these experiences do not seem real to us during times of despair. We exercise our faith in God, "in spite of" the seeming unreality of his existence during despair. Like Job, we maintain our beliefs with our intellectual powers and our thinking abilities despite the events in our lives which seem to communicate chaos and emptiness.

Christian hope is also an important response in the face of meaninglessness. Our hope, during despair, is in God's willingness to reveal himself at some point in our lives. We hope and pray that he will not remain hidden from us, which certainly seems true during despair.

We trust that he will allow us to meet him again in some existentially meaningful experience. We hope in a further disclosure of his power and his love. We hope in continued revelation so that our faith can be undergirded with further experience.

Love, too, can be helpful to the Christian during times of despair. On the one hand, the "faithing" which we do includes having faith that God is loving us and caring for us even though we are not experiencing this love in the present. This can lead us to continue to exercise love in our relationships "as if" our spiritual center did exist and was characterized by love. The place of love in response to meaninglessness is more difficult when our despair is also characterized by estrangement.

Estrangement

The term estrangement has been used to describe the separation which can exist between an individual and God, between an individual and his neighbor, and between an individual and his or her innermost self. This separation may be characterized by indifference and apathy. Estrangement, however, can refer also to alienation, the enmity and hostility which exist in these relationships.

Since God is the center of our existence, estrangement means that we are separated from this center. When humans are out of touch with the center of existence, they may respond with despair. Despair means "without hope" and the person separated and alienated from God and his neighbors experiences hopelessness.

The Christian gospel makes its major thrust at the condition of estrangement by and through its proclamation of love. One meaning of love is "union" and certainly the gospel offers love as a reunion for relationships plagued by separation. Love overcomes separation because it desires fellowship. God's love for us has resulted in his taking initiative toward human beings throughout history in an attempt to establish fellowship. He has responded to our disobedience by both seeking and offering reconciliation. He loved us so much that he gave his only Son to be a messenger of reconciliation.

Hope is a Christian response to estrangement in that our hope is for reconciliation to take place. The despairing person hopes that reconciliation can take place between him or her and God, his or her neighbor, and within his or her own self. This hope enables us to see the possibilities for actualizing what love can accomplish through reunion.

Not Willing to Be a Self

This phrase is used by Søren Kierkegaard to describe a source of despair.[2] I will not use the concept exactly as he does, but his ideas are helpful. God has created each human with potential to become a unique self. Each of us has particular talents and gifts. We each have a unique mind and a unique blend of experience. God has made us with a degree of freedom to become an individual unlike any other. God's gift of life challenges each of us to seek out our destiny, love as he loved, and find our unique identity as a child of God.

Despair often results when we have given up this freedom, sold ourselves into dependency, sacrificed our autonomy, or lost our individuality in the life of another person, group, or institution. When we have buried our talents, choked off our potential, denied responsibility for ourselves, despair often results.

Again, the focus of the gospel proclamation in the face of our unwillingness to be a self is through love. In this instance, we are talking about love of self. Self-love demands self-affirmation. To act, to affirm ourselves is a significant way of participating in the goodness of God's creation. God felt that his creation was good. He has loved man. For us to reject the goodness of ourselves and to fail to love ourselves in appropriate ways is to opt for proclaiming that God's creation, particularly man, is bad or evil.

Being unwilling to be a self is an act of pride in the sense that it elevates our negative feeling about ourselves into a position of truth. However, our faith response to not be willing to be a self is that our selfhood is significant to God. Faith, then, is the "betting our lives" that God created purposefully and knowingly the creatures with which he wanted to have fellowship. Our faith is that the creation is good and that humans are the object of God's love.

Hope is also present in the Christian struggle with despair when it results from failing to be a self. Our hope is that our individuality remains important to God even when we have failed to affirm ourselves in creative ways. Our hope is that God will continue to love us and share his eternal life with us despite our sin and disobedience.

In summary, the Christian who struggles with despair, particularly as despair grows out of meaninglessness, estrangement, and self-negation, does have resources within the Christian faith to call upon in this struggle. Faith, hope, and love are the channels by which the Christian can overcome despair.

I hope this discussion of the Christian faith and depression has been helpful. I hope you will share your perceptions and feelings about the depression you are experiencing with your pastor or with some small group in the church to which you might belong. They can be a source of support and love as you work at escaping the clutches of this spiritual quicksand.

Notes

1. Paul Tillich, *The Courage to Be* (New Haven, Conn.: Yale University Press, 1952), pp. 46-51.

2. Søren Kierkegaard, *The Sickness unto Death*, trans. by Walter Lowrie (Princeton, N. J.: Princeton University Press, 1954), pp. 180-207.

3
Though I Walk Through the Valley
(The Crisis of Dying)

Many of you who are reading this chapter have no reason to suspect that death will soon intrude into your life. You assume that you will grow old and die of natural causes. Other readers may be trying to understand what some family member or friend may be facing because of a terminal illness. I am writing, however, for those readers who are actually facing the possibility or the certainty of an earlier than expected death. I invite the rest of you to eavesdrop.

I wish it were possible to know you personally as I write this chapter. Are you in a hospital bed or at home? Are you sick because your disease has progressed quite far or because of a relapse? Or are you quite well and currently unhampered by any physical symptoms of your disease?

Some of you may know that death is around the corner, others have more time. You may be hoping "they got it all" and "it" might not crop up for another few years. You may be a cancer patient for whom surgery was ineffective because of wide-ranging metastasis and you may be afraid the months will be short. Are you leukemic but presently in remission? Or have you experienced a recurrence of a potentially fatal disease? You may be a person who feels more vulnerable to death upon recovering from a coronary or suffering from kidney failure and hoping for a transplant that might prolong life. You may be quite old and beginning to have a general breakdown of health which you feel is signaling that your body is wearing out. Maybe you are reading this simply because you often think about death. Maybe you fear being killed in an accident, or committing suicide, or dying young like some other member of your family.

Whatever your circumstance, the fact that you would read a

chapter with this title may indicate that you have begun the process of accepting the idea that you are writing the last chapters in your life. I am addressing myself to those who can imagine that they are dying or will die. Those who deny they are terminally ill or have a life-threatening problem probably would not be reading a chapter on dying. I also assume that "making sense" out of this event, relating the reality of death to your Christian faith, is a major concern of your present pilgrimage.

If you are able to face the fact that death for you is no longer "out there" somewhere but lies within the next weeks, months, or years, then you have already come through some painful times. Let's examine some of what you have been through or are going through.

Stages and Phases of Dying

Since dying people do not often talk with one another, you probably have not realized that many things you are experiencing are also experienced by others who are terminally ill or whose health forces them to face the possibility of imminent death. Only in the last fifteen years have professionals in the field of medicine, psychology, and pastoral theology turned their attention to the study of dying. Dr. Elisabeth Kübler-Ross and Rev. Carl A. Nighswonger, two of the pioneers, have helped identify some of the common experiences shared by dying people.[1] We will use some of their research as a guide for our discussion.

Factors Influencing Your Response to Dying

How you respond to the process of dying at this time in your life will depend on many factors. If you have lived a long life and feel like the man who told me, "I have lived most of my years anyway," then you may have less bitterness and resistance than the reader who is young or middle-aged. If you have heavy family responsibilities with spouses and children who depend on you, you will probably have more anger at death and more anxiety about how your death will affect others. If you are a teenager or a young adult just arriving at the threshold of life, you probably feel more cheated than the one who has had opportunities to experience marriage, family, and vocational fulfillment.

If you are a person who is honest with yourself, open to truth, have an appropriate self-acceptance, and live with integrity, you will probably find creative ways of facing your anxieties about dying. When you are able to live a fairly normal routine, your response will be different from those times when you are ill or incapacitated. If the significant people in your life are not coping with your situation, not able to deal openly with it, then it will be more difficult for you to face dying than for those who are able to relate completely and intimately with the significant people in their lives.

Perhaps most importantly, your philosophy of life, particularly your religious beliefs and commitments, will shape your response to dying. We will talk about that in a later chapter.

Shock and Denial

Hearing that you had a fatal or terminal disease was probably a stunning and overwhelming experience, even if you anticipated that the news would be bad. The shock cut deep, immobilized you, and led to a period of numbness. It probably was hard to believe ("Me? Oh, my God, what will I do?"). Your mind may have gone blank, your legs may have gotten weak, you may have cried or gotten very quiet.

Nighswonger calls denial the "emotional shock absorber that allows us to pretend that we did not hear that which we cannot emotionally accept. It is a psychic anesthetic to an otherwise unbearable reality." [2] Denial is our resistance to being consciously aware of, or accepting the fact that, an illness or disease is terminal. It is normal and even necessary to use denial in some form and to some extent when faced with such a trauma. It is an appropriate way of maintaining psychological stability in the face of overwhelming fear and dread. It provides the time to prepare one's inner resources to face an almost unimaginable event.

One reason it is necessary to deny in the beginning is that our unconscious self does not like to consider it possible for us to die.

It is extremely difficult for any of us to imagine our own death. Depth psychologists have taught us that we perceive ourselves as immortal.[3] Of course, we recognize with our intellect that death is universal and that everyone must die, but emotionally we do not imagine ourselves to be included. Weisman calls death "a universal phobia that man tends to believe can be avoided, and avoided again, until, for all he knows, it might be postponed indefinitely." [4] Within this context, of course, death is seen as a bad thing, a negative happening, rather than a normal part of life. Most individuals to whom I minister in the hospital are ill-prepared, bewildered, anguished, and shocked when faced with this reality. This contributes to our resistance to the news. ("Do the tests again, they must have made a mistake." "It can't be, I had a checkup three months ago!")

You have probably swung back and forth between denial, shock, and awareness of the reality you face. This change in feelings will gradually move to the point where awareness is predominant. When the realities begin to filter through, other reactions follow.

Anger

One group of reactions are related to anger and hostility. The angry feelings you have were probably strongest during one phase or period of time, but they may interject themselves again at various times. The hostile reactions include angry feelings over being a victim of fate. The harsh question "Why me?" can be dominant. Why not somebody else who doesn't have a family, or is old and lived a full life, or whose life isn't worthwhile and is a drain on society?

Sometimes anger is projected onto other people. ("I wish it were you instead of me.") Jealousy and resentment of those who do not have the disease often crop up. The feeling of injustice is often expressed. Feeling hurt and frustrated about tasks that are undone, goals that are unaccomplished, loving relationships that will be broken, and responsibilities and promises which will be unfulfilled generates much hostility.

Anger may be expressed to family members, doctors, friends, and nursing personnel. This stage is difficult for others to handle and some will take it personally. Expressing this anger can create a strong sense of guilt.

Anger is often realistic. Perhaps you are angry that friends and relatives have withdrawn from you because of their fears about your illness. Or perhaps you are angry because they did not tell you the nature of your illness earlier, or because you are not being consulted when decisions about treatment are made.

Anger is often directed at God. ("Why has God let this happen?" "If God loved me he would not have this disease affect me." "If God is all-powerful and faith can move mountains, then why doesn't God heal me?" "I have been so good all my life, how could he let this happen to me? It isn't fair!") All these statements reflect the anger and the stress which terminal illness puts on our perceptions of God and our faith relationship.

Bargaining and Negotiating

Another common experience of dying people is the desire to bargain about their fate, to try to make a deal with God. You may have attempted to reach an agreement with God in which you promised something to God in return for an extension of life, relief from pain and suffering, or a miraculous cure. You might have promised to "rededicate your life to God," enter the ministry, do more service through the church, or give more money to Christian causes.

This phase often follows times of strongest anger, particularly anger toward God. Kübler-Ross points out that this bargaining experience may be for some a way of placating God. She uses the illustration of the small child who is told no to some request, throws a temper tantrum and gets angry, but then later tries to be nice and do things that he otherwise would not do in order to win the approval of parents and win a yes in place of the no.[5] During a terminal illness it is easy for a person to revert to this same practice. We may say to God: "Look, I'll be very nice, take my medicine, not be angry at anyone, cooperate with all the doctors and nurses, if only you will extend my life or cure this illness." If you have felt that God has been in some way responsible for your illness, particularly if you feel that you are being punished by God for some thought, deed, or shortcoming in your life, then you will be more likely to feel that if God could be persuaded that you were sorry, he might remove the disease which you feel he sent.

You even may have felt that God was playing games with you, thinking you have done something displeasing to God or failed to do his will in some way, and assume therefore that if you could figure out your mistake God would revoke his curse. Your confession of specific guilts and the desire to provide restitution might influence God to drop his grudge against you.

If you have been "plea-bargaining" with God, it may mean that there are deeper levels of guilt (real or imagined) in your life that you need to explore. Bargaining may also reflect wishful thinking (which is not real Christian hope) that somehow God would be amenable to begging or trade-offs.

If you have believed over the years that you were unacceptable to God and inadequate in his service or if you feel God is displeased or angered with you, then you may not feel you have the right to bargain with God. You probably feel that God's judgment has been rendered on your life and you deserve your fate.

Depression

Depression is another normal experience for dying persons or persons for whom death could be imminent. Depression can be related to several concerns.

One cause can be that the anger one feels about the whole event is turned inward onto the self. So many things elicit anger: treatment procedures, the seeming lack of justice, the jealousy over those who are well and will keep on living, the sense of powerlessness in the face of disease, and the problems your illness is causing for the family. But you can express only so much anger without driving people away. And besides, it seems that there is no real target, no real enemy. Therefore, the anger gets suppressed and turned inward onto the self. Others direct the anger at themselves if they feel partly to blame for their condition, either because of some guilt which brought about punishment or through some irresponsibility which contributed to the illness.

Talking out your hostility and expressing it as completely as possible with someone you trust will help you overcome some of this depression.

You may also experience depression related to grief. For example, you may experience what psychologists term "reactive depression," that is depression in response to the very real losses brought about by hospitalization, treatment procedures, and the illness itself. A woman who has a breast removed may feel she has lost some of her sexuality. It might be the loss of a job that one cannot return to because of the debilitating illness. Losing one's hair, losing the ability to be independent, and losing one's financial security because of the medical bills are all examples of the losses incurred during a severe illness. Reactive depression, then, is a grief response over the losses which accompany the illness.

A deeper type of depression can be those thoughts and feelings about the biggest loss of all, your own self. This depressiveness is caused not by the specific losses previous to death, as in reactive depression, but to the imagined separation from the world at death. As Kübler-Ross notes:

When the terminally ill person can no longer deny his illness, when he is forced to undergo more surgery or hospitalization, when he begins to have more symptoms or becomes weaker and thinner, he cannot smile it off anymore. His numbness or stoicism, his anger and rage will soon be replaced with a sense of great loss.[6]

As a person who is dying, you will need to learn how to express your sorrow for those things which you have lost as well as for those things which you will lose. Expression of this sorrow and bereavement is quite appropriate. You can learn more about grief from reading chapters 6, 7, and 8. Just as it is important for a grieving person to move through their grief to a point of acceptance and affirmation of life, so it is important for you to live through your sorrow so that some acceptance can be reached, some affirmation expressed for life already lived, and some anticipation of resurrection experienced.

Acceptance

At some point in this pilgrimage with a terminal illness, you will hopefully reach a time when you can accept the realities of your situation, gain some reconciliation with death, have the security of "wrapping up your affairs," and reach a place in your significant relationships so that death will bring closure rather than rupture. Your faith can provide the hope and love which undergirds you in the final phases of the process of death so you can experience some fulfillment, security, and comfortableness in the presence of death. You may identify with Kübler-Ross's statement:

If a patient has had enough time and has been given some help in working through the previously described stages, he will reach a stage during which he is neither depressed nor angry about his "fate." He will have been able to express his previous feelings, his envy for the living and the healthy, his anger at those who do not have to face their end so soon. He will have mourned the impending loss of so many meaningful people and places and he will contemplate his coming end with a certain degree of quiet expectation.[7]

It is difficult for some friends, family, and members of the medical staff to respond positively as you relax your grip on life in this stage of acceptance. Since our culture seems to prize those who "fight to the end," it will not be easy for some people to allow you to accept your coming death. Sometimes families and medical staff continue to encourage people to fight for life and make them feel guilty for "giving up." Our frontier spirit makes us feel that "quitting" is sinful. This means that persons who accept their coming death may feel rejected by their family at the end. How much better for you if they can accept your acceptance and be willing to admit that accepting death is an appropriate way for you to handle this last stage of life.

Fears and Anxieties About Death and Dying

Why does death create so much anxiety? One of the major reasons is the amount of fear associated with dying and death. The fact that you get scared out of your mind by the thought of dying does not make you different from others with terminal illness. The sweat-producing, heart-stopping terror that you feel is a natural response to our human limitations, our inability to know what death is and what lies on the other side.

You might remember that Jesus Christ experienced fear and anxiety in the face of death. In the Garden of Gethsemane he became greatly distressed and troubled (Mark 14:33), praying in agony on the ground and sweating profusely (Luke 22:42-44). He told his disciples that his soul was "very sorrowful, even to death" (Mark 14:34) and prayed he would not have to face death (v. 35) and that God would "remove this cup" (death) from him (v. 36). Christians have always believed that God was in Christ, involving himself in the human situation. God understands our fear and anxiety in the face of death because he has experienced this in the person of Jesus Christ.

Yes, it is part of the human experience to fear death, even though this fear will vary from person to person as shaped by their age, health, psychological makeup, previous experiences with death, and religious faith. Fear and anxiety, however, are not the last word. Jesus not only reveals that fear and anxiety about death are real within the human experience, but challenges us with the possibility of responding with hope and courage. He prayed, "nevertheless not my will, but thine, be done" (Luke 22:42) and chose to move ahead with his course of action despite its certain outcome in death. You can evaluate the shape of your own fear and seek within your own faith the hope and courage with which to encounter these fears.

Robert Neale gives a good overview of the types of fears terminally ill people express. He suggests some reasons why people feel these different fears so acutely and points out that our fears of death often reveal our fears about life.[8] Interestingly enough, the moment of death does not seem to be the focus of fear. The main focus is on:

(1) what one loses when death comes, (2) what will happen during the process of dying, and (3) what will happen after death.[9]

Fears and Anxieties Related to What We Will Lose

Separation. We fear separation from our loved ones with whom our lives are so intertwined. The meaning of our existence is in large measure bound up in the web of interpersonal relationships which have been developed over the years, the community of individuals (particularly our own spouses, parents, and children) whom we have loved, around whom we have set our goals, defined our identities, found our security, and experienced our happiness. To lose them is to be terribly alone and vulnerable. We know how emotionally painful grief can be when we lose a relationship. Our own death, however, means losing all these meaningful relationships at one time. No wonder this heavy loss precipitates so much anxiety. To die is to lose a large portion of the meaning of our existence and one of death's major threats is to our perception of whether or not life is meaningful.

Incompleteness and Failure. Like most of us, you have a vocational calling and life goals, including your work, your family, your causes and commitments. Death may keep you from completing some of these tasks and reaching your goals. Our society is oriented toward production, success, and accomplishment. To the extent you have learned to value your life according to these criteria, you will be threatened by your inability to complete the successes and productions you had imagined.

Some reality, of course, is involved in this fear. Will your children be able to go to school? Will your wife be able to manage on her own? Will your husband be able to give the children the emotional support they need? We fear that those we love might be hindered in their future because of our death.

Loss of Control. Some terminally ill people refer to their fear of losing control over their life and destiny. In America, where self-made people are admired and where strong emphasis is given to "pulling your own weight" and "looking out for yourself," many put strong personal value in their ability to master their own destiny. Dying seems to be the opposite and steals control from us.

Fears and Anxieties Related to the Process of Dying

Pain. Most of us are afraid of intense pain, even though we may not have experienced much of it. We commonly believe that dying is painful. This fear is partially valid, since pain can accompany some phases of dying. We fear what pain will do to us, how it will make us act, and how it will affect our loved ones. Modern medicine can control much of our pain, but that in itself creates for some the fear of addiction or the fear that others will think they are weak for not "bearing" the pain.

Indignity. Our culture teaches us that how we present ourselves, both physically and emotionally, is an important part of our selfhood. In hospitals and sickrooms there are odors, tubes, bedpans, unkempt hair, and distorted physical appearance which we think repels our guests. In pain, or during loss of rationality, we fear saying or doing something that would be socially unacceptable and embarrassing in other circumstances. We don't want people to pity us when our bodies show signs of falling before advancing disease.

Dehumanization. Dying patients also fear depersonalization and dehumanization in the process of dying. In hospitals you get handled, punched, pricked, stuck, measured, and poked like an object, often without your prior consent. Sometimes medical technicians forget patients are people, not just bodies. As a result, patients are often left out of what is happening. A patient in our society can lose his or her right to participate in decisions pertaining to treatment. We expect people to take responsibility during their whole life until they begin to die. Then family, friends, and the medical complex take over and treat patients as if they had no mind of their own, no will, and no right to participate in decisions about their life and death. At times he or she even loses the right to receive truthful and complete information. People whisper around patients and then vote on what is best as if the patient were a dependent child. You may fear losing your personhood by being placed on machines.

Being a Burden. Since dying can be a long and expensive process in this day of skyrocketing health care costs, we fear becoming a burden on our families. Socialized medicine or national health insurance has not yet protected all families from the high cost of hospitals, doctors, medicines, rehabilitation centers, and old-age homes. You may fear the financial ruin that your dying could bring to your family. Long, debilitating illnesses also affect schedules, life plans, and the normal activities of those we love. The burden of nursing can be heavy. You may fear the resulting conflicts of anger, guilt, pity, and disgust which can tear families apart.

Becoming unconscious for weeks, when our essential humanness is gone but when biological functioning is continued mechanically, can be a threat to us because of turmoil for our families.

Fears and Anxieties Related to After Death

Although we have data on which to base some of the fears about the process of dying, we do not have much to go on concerning what happens after death.

Fate of the Body. Some people fear what will happen to their bodies after death. They have a difficult time imagining themselves separated or absent from their body and the body being unable to feel or hurt. You may be fearful, therefore, of decay or even of pain from autopsy. You might not be able to imagine leaving your body to a medical school. Because of these fears, Americans spend unnecessary money on caskets, vaults, and "memorial estates" with "good drainage" which are supposed to protect the body.

The Unknown. Some children are afraid of the dark and ghosts. In adulthood some still have more fear of the unknown than the known. Since we have no concrete knowledge of what goes on after death, some people are terrified by their imaginations. To allay this fear some develop exaggerated eschatologies (doctrine of last things) which provide them with step-by-step accounts of what happens after death and seem to transform the unknown into knowns and enable them to allay their fear.

Oblivion. Because the other side of death is unknown, people sometimes fear that it is the "end of the road." People who do not believe in an afterlife may experience anxiety over the fact that their personal existence has come to an end. Believers in an afterlife may also experience this fear even though they are hoping for an afterlife. They ask, "What if the self is tied only to this life and death marks the end of dreams, goals, meanings, and relationships that make up life?" The Christian faith, of course, disagrees with this perception and believes instead in resurrection and eternal life.

Judgment. Western culture is heavily based on religious concepts that include a judgment time after death. Both Catholic and Protestant theology over the centuries has been filled with perceptions of a time for weighing a person's good deeds against their sins. Punishments and rewards are then handed out on the basis of merit. If you have not resolved your feelings about events, actions, or thoughts in your life for which you feel guilty, then this fear may be one of yours.

The Christian faith can play a crucial role in helping you to face these fears and anxieties. It can be the major source of strength and courage as you face the possibilities of an earlier than expected death and provide the hope which makes acceptance of death possible. We will discuss our faith and what it says about death and dying in the following chapter.

Notes

1. Elisabeth Kübler-Ross, *On Death and Dying* (New York: The Macmillan Co., 1969) and Carl A. Nighswonger, "Ministry to the Dying as a Learning Encounter," *The Journal of Pastoral Care*, Vol. XXVI (June, 1972), pp. 86-92.

2. Nighswonger, p. 87.

3. Kübler-Ross, p. 2.

4. Avery D. Weisman, *On Dying and Denying* (New York: Behavioral Publications, Inc., 1972), p. 13.

5. Kübler-Ross, p. 72.

6. *Ibid.*, p. 85.

7. *Ibid.*, p. 99.

8. Robert E. Neale, *The Art of Dying* (New York: Harper & Row, 1973), pp. 24-45.

9. *Ibid.*, pp. 30-35.

4
I Fear No Evil
(The Christian Response to Death)

The Christian faith has believed historically that death is a transition from one reality in the created order to another reality. We note the words of Jesus (John 14:2) that he has gone to prepare another room (a new level of reality) in God's house (all that exists). This is not to say that death is less real, less scary, or not an enemy, as Paul calls it; but it is to say that death is not able to overcome God's love for us (Rom. 8:37-39). Death is a problem for humans. It is the major way in which we are confronted with our finiteness, our limitations of time and space. It is one of the things we know nothing about. Yet, the Christian faith has consistently believed and proclaimed that God's love for us will allow us in some way to transcend death. On what basis does the Christian gospel proclaim such a seemingly irrational hope?

The Nature of Man

The Christian faith believes in the truths communicated by the creation stories of the Hebrews. Regardless of which creation story you read, man is the central figure. In the story as told in Genesis 2:4b-24, the earth already exists. Then God creates man as a "living being" and "planted a garden" for him. Then the rest of the earth is created around man and for man. He is a special creature to God, one with whom God related, with whom he communicated, and with whom he had fellowship. Man's uniqueness is revealed in the fact that no other creature within the creation was suitable as a companion for him in his loneliness. God had to create another human, but of a different sex.

In the creation story told in Genesis 1:1 to 2:4a, man was created last and was given dominion over the earth and expected to fill and subdue it. Here also man is the center of the story. "God said, 'Let us make man in our image, after our likeness'" (1:26). God wanted humans to be different from everything else he created. "So God created man in his own image, in the image of God he created him; male and female he created them" (1:27).

What does being created in the image of God mean? Among other things it must mean that we have a "spiritual personality," the ability to relate to God (in a different way than the rest of creation) and have fellowship with him. Our uniqueness includes possessing some aspect of God's own nature which gives us the potential to communicate with God and experience community with him, as well as with other human beings. However you might interpret the meaning of being created in the image of God, you must believe that as a human being your "personhood" is important in God's eyes. When the psalmist asks, "What is man that thou art mindful of him, and the son of man that thou dost care for him?" (8:4), he answers his own question with the affirmation, "thou hast made him little less than God, and dost crown him with glory and honor" (8:5).

A significant aspect of the Christian belief in eternal life is rooted in this meaning which human beings have for God and the special investment he has made in us.

John Baillie, in his book *And the Life Everlasting*, describes what he calls a "logic of hope." He believes that the Christian hope of eternal life is grounded in man's nature as an individual who can communicate with God and have fellowship with God. He says, "If the individual can commune with God, then he must matter to God; and if he matters to God, he must share God's eternity." [1]

The Nature of God

God Is Love

Why did God choose to create man? The Christian faith has proclaimed that one aspect of God's motivation was related to the loving nature of God. We believe that God desired to create other beings with whom he could have fellowship and communion. The Hebrews believed they were a chosen people with whom God established covenants that included his willingness to love and protect them if they responded with love, respect, and obedience.

The Old Testament is in one sense a history of God's continuing love for the people of Israel. Even when he chastizes them for their disloyalty and disobedience, he is loving and redeeming them.

For you are a people holy to the Lord your God; . . . it is because the Lord loves you, and is keeping the oath which he swore to your fathers, that the Lord has brought you out with a mighty hand, and redeemed you from the house of bondage, . . . Know therefore that the Lord your God is God, the faithful God who keeps covenant and steadfast love with those who love him and keep his commandments (Deut. 7:6-9).

Thus says the Lord: 'The people who survived the sword found grace in the wilderness; . . . I have loved you with an everlasting love; therefore I have continued my faithfulness to you' (Jer. 31:2-3).

The New Testament continues this claim that "God is love" (1 John 4:8,16). This love was revealed in the incarnation. Jesus demonstrated in his life, his relationships, his ministry, and his willingness to suffer on the cross that God loves us. This love is particularly known in God's initiative to bring reconciliation and redemption to the world. "For God so loved the world, that he gave his only begotten Son, that whosoever believeth in him should not perish, but have everlasting life" (John 3:16).

We are so important to God that he has continued to love us despite our resistance. He continues to take initiative toward establishing reconciliation with us despite our rebellion. God loves us enough to provide through the incarnation a special invitation to accept his love. The Christian faith believes that because God loves us so much he would not let those of us who respond to his love be annihilated, but would provide for continued existence and fellowship with him. "See what love the Father has given us, that we should be called children of God; and so we are" (1 John 3:1).

Knowing of God's love, believing in Jesus Christ, and responding by loving God with all that we are, and loving our neighbors as ourselves (Mark 12:30-31), means that we participate in his life.

Whoever confesses that Jesus is the Son of God, God abides in him, and he in God. So we know and believe the love God has for us. God is love, and he who abides in love abides in God, and God abides in him (1 John 4:15-16).

Because Jesus loved so completely, the early Christians knew that God was in this love and believed this love must be of eternal significance. As John Baillie expressed it:

And it was because they knew that God was in the love of Christ that they knew it would last forever. Behind the love of Christ they could discern the love of God, and in that discernment was the pledge of its eternity.[2]

God Is Righteous

Human beings have raised questions about God's integrity for many reasons, the most prominent being the question of why pain and suffering exist. The most important question raised about God's integrity, however, is the question about why God made life subject to death. Leander Keck has said that the key question in the New Testament is:

whether the universal fact of death mocks faith in the living (deathless) God and whether the meaningless agony and dying of the innocent mock the moral integrity of God . . . The central issue is not whether man has an essence that survives death but whether the God in whom he believes, however falteringly, has enough moral integrity to "make good" with the life he himself called into existence.[3]

The historical affirmation and proclamation of the Christian faith is that God is a God of integrity. Our faith is that God will resurrect his people into a new and different existence with him. As William Tuck says about God:

He does not blow out the personality of man as if it were a dime-store candle; he has not placed in our hearts a quest for the eternal to turn around and snatch it from our grasp; he has not created us in his image whimsically to toss us aside as valueless; he has not planted this restlessness within us to extinguish it without a sense of fulfillment.[4]

God's righteousness includes his faithfulness to the promises of redemption. This created order is the province of evil, suffering, injustice, and the last enemy, death. But in God's time the whole creation, including each of us, will be redeemed.

I consider that the sufferings of the present time are not worth comparing with the glory that is to be revealed to us. For the creation waits with eager longing for the revealing of the sons of God; for the creation was subjected to futility not of its own will but by the will of him who subjected it in hope; because the creation itself will be set free from its bondage to decay and obtain the glorious liberty of the children of God. We know that the whole creation has been groaning in travail together until now; and not only the creation, but we ourselves, who have the first fruits of the Spirit, groan inwardly as we wait for adoption as sons, the redemption of our bodies. For in this hope we were saved (Rom. 8:18-24).

Jesus Faced Death with Faith and Courage

In the last chapter we reminded ourselves that Jesus experienced fear and anxiety in the face of death. Since he was fully human, as well as fully divine, his experience can help us accept our own fears and anxieties as a normal human response in the face of death. Fear is not something of which to be ashamed, nor does it mean we are cowardly.

The response of Jesus to his approaching death, however, also challenges us to respond to death with hope. He came away from Gethsemane with a willingness to face death with courage. What provided him with this faith and hope?

The faith of the Jewish people had always been in a living God, a God who was eternal (Ps. 18:46; Hos. 1:10). Not only is God living, he reigns over the earth and all of creation. The Jewish people came to believe that God's sovereignty must certainly include power over death. For example, Jesus would have been familiar with the story about the power of Elijah to restore life (1 Kings 17:17-21).

One event in the life of Jesus, which gives us some insight into the faith which sustained him in the garden, is the conflict with the Sadducees recorded in Mark 12:18-27. The Sadducees denied that there would be a resurrection and asked Jesus a question designed to solicit his agreement. Their question, "whose wife will she be?" suggests that if there was a resurrection, God would contradict his own will. Why? Because in Deuteronomy 25:5, it is suggested that the brother of a deceased husband marry the widow and help her procreate children. If this happened to a woman seven times then who would be her husband in the resurrection? Jesus' answer suggested they were wrong in their beliefs for two reasons: (1) They did not know the Scriptures, and (2) they did not know the power of God (Mark 12:24).

He attacked the Sadducees' premise by pointing out that resurrection does not mean a restoration, or continuation, of life as we know it now. He suggests that resurrection means a transformation of existence in which the meaning of sexuality and marriage will be different. Resurrection will not mean a return to our present state of existence, but will be radically different from life as we know it here.

His second answer refers to the story of the call of Moses in Exodus where God identified himself with the affirmation: "I am the God of Abraham, Isaac, and Jacob" (Mark 12:26). Jesus is pointing out that the text does not say God *was* their God but that he *is* their God. Jesus is suggesting, then, that these patriarchs, although they may exist right now in Sheol, will not remain there forever. God is their God now, which means he is the God of the living; but he will also be their God in the future. Jesus assumes that the hope of resurrection is based on the indestructible relationship of God to his people.[5] He summarized his faith by stating that God "is not God of the dead, but of the living; you are quite wrong" (v. 27).

So Jesus faced death with some of the same uncertainties we do, yet his faith allowed him to trust in the presence of God. His belief that God was the God of the living, gave him hope that death would not have the last word.

The Resurrection

So Jesus was nailed to a cross, died, was buried in a tomb, and then on the third day was resurrected! The power of God had conquered death. A unique event had occurred. This was not a restoration to mortal life, like Lazarus who would later die again, but a transformation! Jesus made several postresurrection appearances to his disciples and various other people before ascending to the right hand of God. Since that time the resurrection has been the central event in the history of the Christian faith. Why?

First, the resurrection established for the disciples beyond any doubt that Jesus of Nazareth was the Christ, the Messiah, God's Promised One. They were certainly not expecting the resurrection, despite some of Jesus' earlier words. They had doubts even at the appearances and needed to see his wounds to make sure it was he. But when the identity was established, the disciples knew that Jesus was Lord.

His resurrection was of a different nature than the restorations to life they had seen before. This meant, secondly, that God had chosen to demonstrate his power in a new way. The incarnation suddenly took on new meaning. God has visited our world in the flesh, lived in a fully human way, died as all men do, but then conquered death. God had demonstrated in an unquestionable way that his love for his creation included life beyond this one!

Thirdly, resurrection meant that Jesus would fulfill his promise to the disciples: "I will not leave you desolate; I will come to you" (John 14:18). Jesus is reunited with his disciples and with all believers down through the centuries. He is now the risen Lord who dwells within his followers.

Most important for those of you who are presently faced with dying and death, the resurrection means that our faith in the God who created and sustains the universe is also the God who "gives life to the dead" (Rom. 4:17). Because of the resurrection we know that God wants us to share in his eternal life. We are to share the "resurrection life" of Jesus who said, "Because I live you will live also" (John 14:19) and "When I go and prepare a place for you,

I will come again and will take you to myself, that where I am you may be also" (John 14:3).

This resurrection life is a quality of life that describes the new relationship possible between man and God. "Therefore, if any one is in Christ, he is a new creation; the old has passed away, behold, the new has come" (2 Cor. 5:17). This new quality of life is available to us in the present. "He who hears my word and believes him who sent me, has eternal life; he does not come into judgment, but has passed from death to life" (John 5:24).

Though this resurrection life is present now, its fulfillment is in our personal resurrection at some future point. We must still face the death that all humans experience. But we face it with the assurance, "God raised the Lord and will also raise us up by his power" (1 Cor. 6:14). We know that our relationship with Jesus means that we are "alive to God" (Rom. 6:11) and that "we shall certainly be united with him in a resurrection like his" (Rom. 6:5).

The earliest Christian proclamations centered around the resurrection of Jesus. In 1 Corinthians 15 we find Paul's strongest arguments for resurrection. There he argues that resurrection was not something restricted to Jesus, but that Jesus' resurrection is our guarantee of what will happen to all Christians.

But in fact Christ has been raised from the dead, the first fruits of those who have fallen asleep. For as by a man came death, by a man has come also the resurrection of the dead. For as in Adam all die, so also in Christ shall all be made alive (1 Cor. 15:20-22).

Paul also speaks strongly about Jesus as the victor over the enemy of death. In resurrection, Jesus has been installed in an office which demonstrates his sovereignty over all creation (vv. 24-25) including a final triumph over death (v. 26).

In this same chapter, Paul describes the "spiritual body" which will be part of the resurrection. Paul believed that "flesh and blood cannot inherit the kingdom of God" (v. 50). The destiny of man cannot be reached with bodies that are subject to death and decay. To have God's goal for humanity fulfilled, we must change from "this mortal nature" and "put on immortality" (v. 53). Paul also points out that at some point in time both the living and the dead will be transformed (vv. 51-52). At that time: "Death is swallowed up in victory. O death, where is thy victory? O death, where is thy sting? . . . thanks be to God, who gives us the victory through our Lord Jesus Christ" (vv. 54-57).

Eternal Life

The concept of eternal life now, is also an important Christian concept for the dying person. The concept is found at several points in the New Testament, but is most strongly stated in the Gospel of John. The Gospel of John presents a somewhat different interpretation of the life and death of Jesus Christ than the other three Gospels. Resurrection is given a minor role and eternal life, which begins in the present, is given the major attention. For example, in the Nicodemus story it is pointed out that a person must be "born anew" to enter into the kingdom of God (3:3-7). Whoever believes in the Son of man "may have eternal life" (vv. 14-15).

The story of Lazarus climaxes the Gospel of John's teaching about eternal life by shifting belief in a future resurrection to believing in Jesus now. When Martha complained that Lazarus would not have died if Jesus had been present (11:21), Jesus promised her that her brother would rise again (v. 23). Martha affirmed that she knew that would be true at the resurrection on the last day (v. 24), but Jesus said: "I am the resurrection and the life; he who believes in me, though he die, yet shall he live, and whoever lives and believes in me shall never die" (vv. 25-26). The point being that whatever may happen to the dead in the future, belief in Jesus Christ brings life of an eternal quality in the present.

This makes John's Gospel different from Paul's letters which emphasize resurrection at some future point. Unlike the Pauline position, which states that flesh and blood cannot inherit the kingdom of God and therefore a transformation is necessary at the end of time, John's Gospel insists that the kingdom of God can be inherited in the "now" because the Spirit provides a new dimension of life. Eternal life is a quality of life, not a quantity. In short, the Gospel of John suggests that those who believe and have faith in Jesus Christ do not ever come under the power of death, but pass from death into life in the present. That is not to say that death is not real. It is to claim that death does not have ultimate power and affirms that the believer continues to live even though he dies!

In Summary

The author of 1 John writes that our faith in the God of love, and our assurance that God lives in us and that we participate in his eternal life, gives us "confidence for the day of judgment" (4:17). The day of death will come for all of us, but "there is no fear in love, but perfect love casts out fear" (4:18). We can face death with trust that God will take care of us, that he created us for fellowship, and wills to maintain communion with us. The author of 1 John sums up his reasons for writing this letter by saying, "I write this to you who believe in the name of the Son of God, that you may know that you have eternal life" (5:13). This was the assurance of the early Christians and is no less for us today. As Paul so magnificently summarized:

Who shall separate us from the love of Christ? Shall tribulation, or distress, or persecution, or famine, or nakedness, or peril, or sword? . . . No, in all these things we are more than conquerors through him who loved us. For I am sure that neither death, nor life, nor angels, nor principalities, nor things present, nor things to come, nor powers, nor height, nor depth, nor anything else in all creation, will be able to separate us from the love of God in Christ Jesus our Lord (Rom. 8:35-39).

Notes

1. John Baillie, *And the Life Everlasting* (London: The Epworth Press, 1961), p. 163.
2. *Ibid.*, p. 49.
3. Leander E. Keck, "New Testament Views of Death," in Liston O. Mills, ed., *Perspectives on Death* (Nashville: Abingdon Press, 1969), pp. 97-98.
4. William P. Tuck, *Facing Grief and Death* (Nashville: Broadman Press, 1975), p. 90.
5. See Keck, pp. 38-42.

5

For Thou Art with Me
(Overcoming the Sting of Death)

Facing your coming death has been difficult, but accepting the reality has given you an opportunity to bring your life to a close in a manner that many do not have. Choosing to make dying a part of your living can now lead to responsible decisions which can greatly affect your family and other significant people in your life. Fulfillment may seem a strange word for some, yet you have that possibility in the remaining time.

Of course how many of the following ideas and suggestions are really possible for you depends on the nature and progress of your illness and the amount of physical and emotional energy you have at your command. Those of you who are in remission, functioning fairly normally, and seem to have many months in front of you, can consider all these ideas. Others of you may be quite ill from the disease, with decreased energies and seemingly less time, which limits your ability to consider some of the possibilities below.

Responsible Decisions

Teaching Toward Independence. If you are a husband or wife who will leave a dependent family, you can teach them to do things for which you usually take responsibility. A mother can teach husband and children to cook, run the appliances, shop, sew, and clean. Husbands can teach things about keeping books, running lawn-mowers, maintaining cars. You may know things or have taken responsibility for things within your church, your club, or for older members of your family, which someone else needs to learn about so they can take over at the appropriate time. Teaching people to fill your shoes after your death can be a very rewarding and helpful way of bringing completion into your dying.

Love and Intimacy. Your openness toward your death and the stability of your faith can make you and the most significant people in your life open to the living which is left. How wonderful for you if this honesty and openness can lead you and your spouse, your children, your parents, and other close friends to newer and deeper levels of intimacy. It will be nice to experience the peace and understanding which comes with it and can add to your feeling of completion and fulfillment. Expressing your needs, fears, hopes, and doubts will provide bonds of closeness which will reduce some of the fear and encourage you in your encounter with death.

Reconciliation in Relationships. During your life some relationships with meaningful people, like parents, adolescent children, in-laws, colleagues, and fellow church members, may not have turned out well. You have an opportunity to take initiative toward those with whom you have felt separation, alienation, anger, suspicion, or misunderstanding. You may be able to describe your feelings to them, express your anger, confess your guilts, forgive them, and establish an understanding that will allow love to flow freely between you. This will be particularly helpful if you feel guilty about the way you have related to a particular person. Most of us feel more mature, more at ease with ourselves, and more in tune with God when we can turn broken relationships into whole ones. Usually we put it off until tomorrow, but that won't work for you.

Confession and Forgiveness. Taking stock of your life may also reveal other events, people, thoughts, or actions, about which you feel sinful, inadequate, or a failure. Evaluating these historical pieces of your life and confessing your role in each of them, will enable you to ask forgiveness from God and from those affected (if they are available). Your pastor or some other trusted minister or friend would willingly share this part of your pilgrimage.

Putting Your Affairs in Order. Like many people, you may never have made a will. Now you will want to evaluate carefully how you wish to have things taken care of after your death. If you have an immediate family (spouse and children) it will probably be simple to decide "who" receives your possessions. Attention can be given to helping the surviving spouse plan how to use the possessions. If you are a husband, for example, you may wish to have lengthy conversation with your lawyer, your insurance agent, and your wife to make sure of complete agreement and understanding about the will and how insurance payments will be handled. It is also good for the surviving spouse to update his or her will to be sure that children are protected in event of his or her death.

If you are young with no family of your own, or older with your family scattered and no spouse, or divorced and not remarried, the "who" and "what" of a will is more flexible. Feeling that your possessions will be making appropriate contributions to people's lives and that you will be loving a while longer through what you leave, is a good feeling.

Financially you can make other decisions such as paying off or consolidating debts, changing ownership of belongings, changing money into other bank accounts, teaching the survivor about your holdings, or selling a business that could not be run without you that will solidify and simplify your family situation after your death.

Your Funeral. It is meaningful to some persons to plan their own funerals. What would you like for your funeral service to communicate about you and your family? What will you want your family to experience? What will they need? This preparation by you, your pastor, spouse, and children can give the family a chance to participate in making your death a transition, not chaos. Other questions about events immediately after your death have to be dealt with: do you want to be cremated, leave your body to a medical school, allow parts of your body to be transplanted and contribute to the ongoing life of other persons, have an autopsy? These decisions can be made in open discussion with your loved ones, taking everyone's needs and fears seriously. If you and your spouse, perhaps even older children, can choose cemetery plot and casket in advance, it will save your family some stress and you can be more economically realistic in your decision. Choosing the funeral home and talking with the director about arrangements can also be helpful.

Planning Final Stages. Your physician and your closest family members can be engaged in conversation about the final stages of your illness. The physician will know how to describe the various possibilities, and decisions can be made about it in advance. How much pain do you want to endure? Is addiction going to be a problem? How long should you be kept alive after you lose consciousness for the last time? What about heroic measures? Will the family be allowed to be present? Are the final stages such that you can be at home, or would this be too hard on the family? In these conversations you and your family can clearly convey your wishes to the doctor and develop your trust in his or her ability and willingness to accept your needs and values. Knowing your willingness to face and accept these ultimates will allow him or her to deal realistically with you and your family. If for any reason you cannot trust your doctor to allow you and your family to participate in this decision-making, then ask for a referral to a physician who will! You have the right to have medical care that takes your thoughts and feelings seriously!

Suicide. It will disturb some to have this word appear, but the truth is that some of you have considered, or will consider, suicide. You may have considered this as a response to your fears about a long dying process, particularly fears about pain, suffering, surgery, or mutilation. Others think of suicide as a way of protecting their family against the emotional and financial stress of prolonged illness or debilitating disease which can lead to "being a vegetable." Taking your life can be a way of striking back at fate or at God for allowing or causing this illness. Other people wish to have more control over their dying and death rather than leaving it to the attacking illness. Believing that your family and physician cannot tolerate helping you have a quiet, dignified death, may also lead you to consider taking your life.

In any case, you need to think carefully about what these thoughts of suicide mean to you and your family. Talk it over with a trusted friend, chaplain, counselor, or pastor. Explaining your feelings and thoughts may reveal the causes and motivations for your desire to take your own life. It will give you an idea of what aspects of your dying have not been resolved, understood, or controlled. Remember, however, that many of the particular things which you think could be solved by taking your own life may also be worked out between you and your family, your doctor, and your minister if you take the initiative to share these concerns with them.

It will be important to think of the consequences suicide would have on your family. They are the ones who may feel shame, rejection, hurt, and guilt. They are the ones who will have to deal with what people will say and think.

Historically the Christian faith has considered suicide a breach of the commandment, "You shall not kill" (Ex. 20:13). In this context suicide is considered a violation of God's privilege to take life and is therefore a sin. Other Christians approach the question from a different perspective, believing that God expects us to take responsibility for our dying as well as our living. They do not believe God has any investment in prolonged suffering and the dehumanization of debilitating illnesses. You must decide from within your own Christian faith what you think about suicide.

Relating to Family and Friends

One dilemma you face as you struggle toward acceptance of the coming death is deciding how to relate to the significant people in your life. You are expressing and working through your own thoughts and feelings in ways which will help you deal with death in an appropriate manner and in accordance with your system of values. To do this adequately demands relating openly and honestly to family and friends. It would be nice if they could accept your situation, your fears and anxieties, your desire to talk it over and feel comfortable walking with you through "the valley of the shadow of death." In actuality, however, many of these significant people are tremendously upset and threatened by your situation. They will relate to you in a variety of ways.

Some play the "denial game," pretending they do not know about your terminal illness. Others will acknowledge to themselves that you have a terminal illness but will pretend you either don't know or don't want to talk about it. They try to relate to you as if nothing is different. They are always cheerful, avoid any reference to death and dying, and find it difficult to be serious when in your presence for fear that the dreaded subject will surface. Some of those closest to you will not allow themselves to consciously believe you are terminally ill. They will deny the seriousness of the situation even to themselves.

Other friends and family members will be so frightened by your dying that they will leave you alone. You may be surprised how many friends and relatives are unable to cope with you as a dying person. They withdraw and avoid contact. They do not visit as often and do not invite you to their homes. They may treat you as if you had something contagious and attempt to avoid contact with you, perhaps even with your family.

People will project their anxieties onto you and be fearful that talking about your situation with any seriousness might break you down in tears or cause an emotional upheaval. They are fearful of adding to your emotional pain. They also feel a sense of helplessness, because in our society we have no idea how to relate to dying people. They will particularly feel this way during your bouts with anger and depression. Your situation reminds them of their own vulnerability and human limitations; and as we have already indicated, most people do not want to think about that reality. Avoiding you will protect them from this stress.

Problems may have developed between you and your family during the early stages when you were dealing with denial and shock. It might have been difficult for your family to let you know the diagnosis. If the truth was kept from you for a long time (despite direct requests), you may be angry at those who hid the truth. Or you may have protected them from your suspicions for a long time, worrying about how they would respond. Arguments may have taken place over what course of treatment to choose. Embarrassment, protectiveness, denial, anxiety, fear, and anger may all have interfered with communication in the earlier phases.

Now, communication, trust, and openness will have to be re-established. Since it will be important for you to plan your family's future, make appropriate farewells, and bring some completeness into your life, it will be necessary to initiate the subject of your death with some of these people. You will find yourself working at making them comfortable, even though it would seem the opposite should be true.

You will expect to get significant help from your doctor and your pastor in working through the emotional problems of being terminally ill. Many of these professionals are quite able to facilitate a dying person's struggle, share with you in the pain and suffering, help interpret thoughts and feelings to family and friends, and share their own wisdom with you. They will not be afraid of the realities of life and death and are able to integrate humanness into their professional functioning. However, doctors are trained to promote life and are introduced early to treating bodies instead of people. For many doctors death is the enemy, and they don't like to lose. Some might be more afraid of death and find more of a need to deny it than you do.

Pastors may also deny the reality of death and the realistic problems of the terminally ill person. They can make you feel that your faith should prevent you from having any of the multiple thoughts and concerns with which you are wrestling. If either physicians or pastors have not dealt with their own personal feelings about death, it might be even more important for them to deny some of the realities of your situation. They may use "busyness" to avoid you and use medical or religious jargon as a way of keeping conversation from the deep feelings you are experiencing.

In all cases, however, you will be able to find some friends and family members who are mature enough to cope with the fact that you are dying! They will be able to be open and honest in their response. They will feel free to share their own thoughts and feelings about your death with you and listen carefully to the many experiences about which you would like to communicate. They will appreciate your need to talk and will be able to laugh with you when you are happy and cry with you when you are sad. They will recognize that you know much more about human limitations than they have yet faced and will be willing to learn from you. I hope you will seek these people out and spend many hours sharing with them. They can be of inestimable help to you over these weeks and months, and you can contribute to their understanding of both life and death.

6

Someone You Love Is Dying!
(The Crisis of Anticipatory Grief)

A significant crisis for any of us is the shocking news that someone we love, or with whom we have been significantly related, has an incurable illness or a life-threatening disease. In our time medical science allows us to know in advance that certain diseases and illnesses are fatal, even though modern medicine may slow them down or even bring long periods of remission. We live with the phrase "terminal illness" to describe these diseases which will bring an earlier than expected death.

We establish many meaningful relationships in our lives. They provide us with security, love, affection, stability, and contribute to our personal identity. When these relationships are threatened, by serious illnesses for example, we automatically feel anxious. When these illnesses become life-threatening, or are judged to be terminal, our anxiety is multiplied.

What is Anticipatory Grief?

In chapter 7 we have described bereavement grief as the intense emotional and physical response to the loss by death of a person with whom one had a significant emotional relationship. Anticipatory grief refers to our emotional and physical response when we know one of the significant people in our life will die or is threatened by death. Anticipatory grief, therefore, refers to grief which occurs prior to a specific loss, as distinguished from the bereavement grief which occurs after a loss. Anticipatory grief is the process we experience to prepare ourselves ahead of time for a significant loss. It is the process of getting ready for a difficult and traumatic event. Anticipatory grief, like bereavement grief, takes place anytime there is a threatened loss of something important in our lives, such as making a geographical move, losing a child to marriage, or having a loved one go into the Armed Forces. However, in this chapter we will be focusing on anticipatory grief which occurs when we are threatened by the probable death of a person we love.

The Importance of Anticipatory Grief

Before going further, we must accept that many people do not allow themselves to participate in anticipatory grief. Phyllis Silverman, in her study of widows, found that many did not grieve in advance even though they were aware of their husband's terminal illness.[1] When interviewed after the death, most of these widows felt they had not fully accepted the reality of their situation until the actual moment of death. They had learned to live with the illness from which their husbands suffered and did not begin to mourn until the door was finally closed by death. One of my students knew his mother had terminal cancer for four years. After her death, he said that he had not really allowed himself to experience anticipatory grief, with all of its emotional components, even though he had prepared intellectually for her death.

It is also true that some professionals have questioned whether or not the experience of anticipatory grief is helpful. Some believe that anticipatory grief, when fully experienced, contributes to a more lengthy bereavement grief. Silverman, for example, thinks that if wives of terminally ill husbands mourned prior to their husband's death they would have difficulty functioning adequately.[2]

Other professionals, however, feel that participation in anticipatory grief is a healthy experience. Carl Nighswonger, for example, believes that effective anticipatory grief work decreases the possibility of delayed or morbid grief reactions following the actual death of a loved person.[3] He recognizes that anticipatory grief does not prevent the necessity of experiencing bereavement grief. He believes, however, that handling the conflicts in anticipatory grief makes bereavement grief much easier and healthier. I am convinced by my own experience that if you participate fully in the experience of anticipatory grief you will be better able to handle the grief which follows the death.

More important, however, I believe if you appropriately recognize and face your anticipatory grief, you will be more likely to relate in mutually meaningful ways with the person who is dying. Nighswonger and his colleagues in the "Death and Dying Program" at the University of Chicago Hospitals found that when the anticipatory grief of the family was openly experienced at the same time the dying person was openly dealing with his or her grief, then the dying person was much better able to accept the situation and face death with dignity and an attitude of peacefulness. Nighswonger called this mutual acceptance "a tribute to the capacity of the human spirit to respond to life's crucial encounters with dignity, meaning, and purpose." [4]

Certainly this ideal cannot be reached when either the patient or the family denies the realities of the situation or is too frightened to face the realities openly with the other. Many social taboos inhibit families from sharing the fact of an impending death with one another. However, it can be very meaningful when people who love each other openly talk about their fears and share concerns about the fact that death will soon separate them and interrupt their relationship in this world. On the other hand, it is a sad experience for a chaplain to watch, for example, a husband and wife who have shared many of life's intimacies pretend during the final weeks that one of them is not dying. The dying person tries to protect the survivor by not revealing that he or she knows of the impending death. The survivor pretends that death will not really come and acts as if the patient is not aware of the impending death. Both are fearing the amount of emotional pain the other might experience if they openly shared the reality of the situation.

In our society, another hindrance to openness about dying is our fear of becoming emotional with each other. Your fear of "breaking down" may keep you from sharing with your loved one the deepest fears and anxieties you are experiencing during this crisis. Failing to share these feelings, however, also prohibits you from sharing the positive feelings of love, compassion, and gratitude for the life you have had together.

If you are experiencing anticipatory grief you have an advantage over the person who experiences grief over a sudden or unexpected death. You have the opportunity to communicate to your loved one all the things that you would have liked to have communicated if the person had died suddenly. You have the opportunity to affirm your love, express appreciation for the life you have shared together, and share mutual hopes and dreams.

The Process of Anticipatory Grief

Your emotional reaction to learning of the terminal illness of your parent, spouse, child, or close friend is much the same as he or she is experiencing. (See chapter 3.) The initial reaction is one of shock, characterized by a numbness which seems to freeze one's body, mind, and spirit. Some experience immediate panic and a feeling of "falling apart." Denial and disbelief will be present for a while, maybe a long while, depending on many factors, such as the depth and meaning of the relationship to the person who has the life-threatening illness.

Later, as recognition of the reality sinks in, you will probably experience episodes of anger. You too will ask "why." You will question creation's justice, wonder how this could happen to someone "as good as he is," and why it couldn't have happened to someone else who didn't matter. You may be angry at God for causing it or for not preventing it. I hope your faith will make it possible for you to express these feelings openly with and toward God, realizing that God understands your anger and is not threatened by it.

Bargaining with God is as easy for you to do as your loved one. You may promise God to be a better Christian, to give more money, or to fulfill some long-forgotten promise if healing could occur. Through these and other ploys you may try to "buy God off." If you feel that somehow you are responsible for this illness striking your loved one, you may bargain with God to punish you rather than the dying person. Or you may confess your guilt and offer to try to make amends if God will remove his judgment from this loved one. One of my colleagues, whose sister died when he was a teenager, has shared how guilty he felt because of his worry that her cancer was God's way of punishing him for his adolescent sexual fantasies. It is difficult to imagine that the God who loves us would cause someone else to suffer for our failures and shortcomings.

Depression and despair will also intrude. Periods of feeling low, "blue," "down," and sad will occur. Part of this despair will be related to the losses you begin to anticipate: plans which will not be fulfilled, goals not reached, and security taken away. One young married woman shared that one of her lowest points during her father's illness was when she realized that he would never see her children. The most significant loss, of course, will be the loss of the person who is dying. Anticipation of the void left by his/her departure and the vague fears about what his/her absence will mean to your life is depressing.

You may also experience some of the same responses people have in bereavement grief (grief which occurs *after* a loss). A full account is given in chapter 7, but here are some ways these responses occur in anticipatory grief.

The shock and numbness we have described already. Your fantasies will include positive episodes in which the loved person is well again and life will be as usual or even better. Other fantasies will be negative and include images about their death, the how, when, and where of it. Some fantasizing may focus on what you will do after the loved one dies. Your dreams may include references to whom you might remarry, having more children, or how you will use insurance money. This is one way your self prepares for the death.

Flashbacks of bygone years will provide memories of the relationship you have enjoyed. Some memories will be on the negative aspects of the relationship and may lead to some experience of guilt.

You have probably experienced "floods of grief," weeping intensely in anticipation of your loss. At these times the pain, hurt, loss, anger, and fear mix into a gigantic surge of tears which express the heaviness of this human dilemma.

As both the chapter on acute grief and the chapter on dying indicate, the final stage of anticipatory grief can be a tentative acceptance of the reality that death will claim this person with whom your life has been so significantly interwoven. Acceptance means coming to terms with our human situation, our limitations of time and space, and our vulnerability to disease. Acceptance does not mean to like what is happening but to realize that in this corner of God's creation, pain, suffering, and death are inescapably involved in our lives. It is to face the limitations of our humanness with faith that God is still in control.

It is much easier to deal rationally with the coming loss and accept it intellectually than to understand and accept it at emotional levels. Our rational self is reconciled more easily than our emotional self. As death draws closer, new emotions stir and deeper levels of awareness and resistance are tapped. Grief may become acute again; and you may be forced to cry out anew, "No, it isn't so!" or in anger to declare again, "It isn't fair!" Acceptance may always be relative to the particular level at which you have been able to consciously think and feel about your coming loss.

As in bereavement grief, the process of anticipatory grief does not move smoothly through exact stages. It is rather unique for each individual depending on many factors. The length, depth, intensity, and character of your anticipatory grief may be shaped differently from that of another. These phases mentioned above may come in any order and will certainly come in all conceivable mixtures. You will swing back and forth through these phases day-to-day and week-to-week. As Reeves says, this repetition is not meaningless:

It means that the realization of impending loss strikes at deeper and deeper levels as the time draws near, and at each deeper level the process, which seemed earlier to have been accomplished, must be worked through again.[5]

The fact that you might find yourself flowing back and forth among these stages of grief does not mean you have not dealt with grief adequately or even that you have regressed. It may simply mean that your grief has been touched at a newer level because of a deeper awareness of yourself and/or the dying person.

A difference between anticipatory grief and bereavement grief is related to the "acceleration" of the emotions. Under usual circumstances bereavement grief begins with an intense emotional shock, then over a period of time the intensity of the grief begins to diminish. Anticipatory grief, however, begins with a smaller shock and then increases in intensity as the time of actual loss approaches.

The Dynamics of Anticipatory Grief

Anger. We have described how anger is a normal part of grief. (See pp. 17, 36.) In anticipatory grief this anger is also present and can be directed in many of the same ways toward doctors, other family members, fate, God, or the disease. Some of this anger will be valid, but it will also be fueled by your response to the threat which death poses to you. It is a "fight" reaction toward an enemy— death.

In anticipatory grief, however, anger also gets focused on the person who is dying. It is embarrassing for you to feel this anger, and yet you can't escape it. It seems contrary to your love for the dying person. It is irrational and seems disloyal, but it is part of the emotional experience.

This anger may focus on time. It is easy in the latter stages of an illness to wish for the dying person to hurry up and die. When the illness drags on and on, when the person seems constantly on the verge of death but keeps pulling through, when hospital bills pile up and economic anxiety runs high, when schedules and life-styles are strained to the breaking point, and when everyone is tired, it is easy for anger to surface.

Anger at the dying person for dying is also irrational, yet it is easy for the spouse or children who will remain to feel abandoned and deserted. "If he really loved us he wouldn't die." Anger can be expressed because the patient will not take medicine or follow other therapeutic instructions. Resentment can arise because of the heavy burden which nursing the patient puts on the family. Family members also experience anger because their whole life seems put "on hold" while the loved one is dying.

When death or separation does not take place when anticipated, it can create many difficulties in the interpersonal relationships of those who anticipated a separation. James Knight reports the case of a university faculty member, suffering from Hodgkins disease, whose illnesses relating to this disease required hospitalization for weeks and months over a ten-year period. During these periods of hospitalization, he was not expected to recover; but in each case he had a remission. When he returned home, it was always a highly charged, negative atmosphere. He felt much hostility, resistance, and lack of intimacy from his wife and children. This was confusing to both him and the family until they realized that each time he went to the hospital they anticipated his death and began grieving as if he would die. They were getting themselves emotionally ready to live without him. When he lived, they had to make a quick readjustment when he returned home, a readjustment that was difficult. Without realizing it they resented the fact that he lived and made it necessary for them to readjust to his life after they had tried to adjust to his death.[6]

Guilt. As with hostility, guilt is usually involved in grief. (See pp. 18 ff.) In anticipatory grief, guilt is often related to the experiences of anger mentioned above. It doesn't seem natural to be angry at the patient. Family members cannot imagine being so insensitive as to wish for a loved one to die. It doesn't seem very loving to be so concerned with money or with your own schedule. It doesn't seem Christian to feel so thwarted. When these thoughts do occur, therefore, guilt may not be far behind ("How could I think such a thing?").

When death will be a welcome visitor and bring relief from pain and suffering, the hope family members have for a quick and easy death does not produce as much guilt.

You may feel guilty about your failures in the relationship and regret that things have not been better. You may even feel guilty that you are surviving—feeling it should be you who was dying rather than this particular loved one. You may feel guilty about not relating as creatively as you think you should to the dying person during their illness. Or, you may feel guilty that you cannot "do something" to bring about a reduction in suffering.

Hope. Hope in bereavement grief cannot focus on living because death has already occurred; but in anticipatory grief, this is not so. Hope normally focuses first on life itself. As you go through anticipatory grief, it is difficult not to hope that a wrong diagnosis was made, that the prognosis will not be bad, that a miracle cure might be found in time, or that extra months or years will be added to those expected by the medical staff. Until the final stages of anticipatory grief, it is our hope that somehow the loss can be delayed or even prevented. Sometimes the hopes are unrealistic from the start, sometimes they are not; but they still affect the anticipatory griever. Hope gets mixed up with denial and bargaining with God in a different way than is possible in bereavement grief.

Hope is very important to you and the dying person. Hope must be related to the realities, yet focused on the day-to-day possibilities. It is appropriate to hope that in your situation the medical treatment will be effective. When the physical evidence indicates otherwise, hope must be focused in a new direction or hope will not give meaning.

In the final stages, the families' experience of hope will ideally shift from continued life to making the most out of the lifetime which is left. Hope in the final stages can focus, not on prolonged life, but on the realistic possibilities of facilitating a death which allows as much fulfillment as possible under the circumstances. Hope should give attention to freeing the dying person from unnecessary pain and suffering, protecting them from loss of personhood, and allowing death with dignity. Most of all our hope can be centered in the goodness of God and our faith that all things ultimately make sense, despite the fact that our human limitations obscure our understanding. We trust that the God who loves us will take care of us and our loved ones even in times of trauma such as dying and death.

Fear. Like your loved one who is dying you too will be afraid, but your fears will focus on some different things. You will experience fear about how other people will react to the dying and the death. One friend was fearful about how his mother would be able to handle his sister's long-term illness. Would she break down physically or emotionally from the long strain? Fears are expressed by others in such words as: "How can I handle the children by myself?" "How will I support the family?" Other fears focus around how much pain the loved person will have to endure, fear that one would be inadequate to handle a medical emergency, fear that one might not relate in the most creative way to the person who needs them, fear of not being present at the moment of death (or of being present), and fear about the dying person's relationship to God.

Relating to the Dying Person

The major focus of your attention during this period of time, of course, will be on the significant person in your life who is dying. But how do you relate? What can you do or say? Difficult questions at best and you will have to find your own answers, but we can point in a few directions.

Telling the Truth. The most difficult question usually comes first. "Should we tell him/her?" I must not hide my own bias that every terminally ill person has the right to know, if they so desire, the realities about their physical situation. I believe they should be given an opportunity to know the nature of their illness, the possibilities that lie ahead, and the results of treatment procedures. To me it is unfair to try to keep people from participating in such a significant part of life, namely, their own dying!

Reasons for not being honest with persons who have a life-threatening illness are usually that they "couldn't take it," it would "upset" them, or they would have an "emotional breakdown." All these things are possible; after all it is no easy thing to face death. But to protect people from being upset is not necessarily the way to contribute to a whole and human existence. We must face the fact that in most instances the family and physicians do not tell people the whole story because of their own fears and anxieties about dying and death and their own inability to handle someone else's fears and anxieties about it.

Plenty of research indicates that most dying people become aware of their situation anyway, even if they never allow the family to know that they know.[7] One of the saddest games played by patient and family is the mutual pretending that nothing is really wrong. Denial is one thing, but pretending is another. The dying person tries to protect his family by not revealing that he knows of the impending death and has many concerns about it. The family also pretends that death is not coming and that they have no fears and anxieties about it. Neither realizes that fears and anxieties are not as bad when shared with people we care about.

Hiding the true diagnosis may keep a person from using his remaining life as responsibly as possible and may deprive him of opportunities to bring closure to life. Isn't that stealing? Refusing to give information, telling untruths, or denying that you know anything when your loved one directly asks is, in my opinion, a breach of love's commitment.

The other side of this must be discussed. Some people will not want to know everything and will prefer to stay in the stage of denial. Therefore, I think that our responsibility is to *give opportunity* for persons to know the realities, leaving room for them to close the door after you open it.

If the person for whom you are grieving cannot or will not begin to accept and deal with the realities of their illness, then you have no choice but to wait. Hopefully, the day will come when they begin moving out of the denial stage into the process of acceptance. Meanwhile, you need to find someone with whom you can talk about the multitude of thoughts and feelings reverberating through you—a pastor, nurse, physician, or friend who can listen, understand, reflect, and comfort.

Sharing the Process of Dying and Grieving

If your loved one moves toward acceptance then he or she will be going through much of the same process you have been experiencing. Certainly many taboos exist that will make it uncomfortable for both of you to talk about dying, death, and grief. If you push through these taboos, however, you can help bring a meaningful closure to your relationship and to his or her life. It is quite appropriate for two people who have been intimately involved with each other over the years to share with one another the fears, anxieties, angers, and guilts that are surfaced by the fact that death will soon separate them and interrupt their relationship. While it is certainly true that you will not be of much help to the terminally ill person if you are constantly upset and emotional while with them, it is also true that the sharing of emotional experiences, the feelings which are engendered by your knowledge of their situation, and the anticipatory grief that you are experiencing is quite appropriate. Many memories need to be relived, decisions made, gratitude expressed, confessions spoken, forgiveness given, and love shared. You have the opportunity to close out the relationship in ways that those who suffer sudden grief wish they had.

Loneliness and fear of separation are major experiences in both dying and in grief, but these can be overcome by close relationships and community. Dealing openly and realistically with the situation can decrease many of the fears and anxieties of both the dying person and you who are experiencing anticipatory grief. For you and this loved person to share these thoughts and feelings can be a significant part of the relationship which you have enjoyed. Bringing closure to your relationship and affirming the relationship that has existed can enable your loved one to die with a sense of peace and tranquility that he could not manage if he were alone, isolated, or unable to share his grief with someone who cares for him.

Presence. One important fact in relating to the dying person is to remember that one of his fears relates to being abandoned. Studies show that the professional people who take care of the terminally ill cut down on the amount of time which they spend with terminally ill people as the illness progresses and death approaches. This is also true of family members and friends. If you are successfully working through your grief response and have the maturity to do so, it would be important to be present as often as possible with the terminally ill person and to give assurances that your willingness to be present is not compromised by your anxieties over the advancing disease. The fear of loneliness is a related fear of the terminally ill person. Your presence and your willingness to verbalize with them concerning both profound things and day-to-day things will aid them in their process of dying.

Contributing to Completion. As the dying person for whom you are grieving moves to a position of acceptance, he will hopefully give time and attention to making responsible decisions about his death. Bringing order and completion to his life situation enables him to feel some fulfillment. Hopefully your own acceptance of his approaching death will allow you to participate with him in putting his affairs in order, writing wills, settling financial problems, planning for insurance receipts, planning the funeral, and making decisions about organ donations and autopsy. (See pp. 57 f.) The dying person can also share with you the spiritual concern, doubt, hope, and faith with which he is wrestling.

When Death Comes

When the death you have expected actually comes, your anticipatory grief comes to an end. The loss you have dreaded, dreamed about, and feared (or in other cases hoped and prayed for) has finally happened; and the reality of the loss must be faced. Anticipatory grief is different in several ways from bereavement grief. The end point of the two types of grief is different. The length of bereavement grief is based on the nature of the loss, the intensity of the relationship, the type of death or loss that took place, and the psychological makeup of the individual griever. It may last for months to years. However, in anticipatory grief the end point is set by the actual occurrence of the anticipated loss. Anticipatory grief, then, comes to an end at the moment the loss occurs. Grief, of course, usually continues; but as bereavement grief, not anticipatory grief.

If you have been adequately, openly, and realistically dealing with anticipatory grief, your experience with bereavement grief will be different at some points from those whose loss is unexpected. The shock will not be as intense; the disbelief will either be nonexistent or last a shorter time. The emotional numbness phase will probably not be characterized by as much "emotional frozenness" nor last as long. Some of the struggles between fantasy and reality will have already occurred, and the shape of your fantasies will be different. In short, the bereavement grief will not be quite as intense nor as lengthy if you have participated in anticipatory grief. Your experience of personal resurrection will happen more quickly.

We must hasten to say, however, that to expect the grief to be easy, or in some sense mostly finished, is probably unrealistic. Most of the people I have worked with as a pastor or chaplain still feel an emotional impact at the time of death. This is particularly true when the dying person had not lived a full life or when the illness progressed rapidly at the end. The impact is not as great if the dying person has been in a great deal of suffering over long periods of time or has been unconscious and unaware of the environment because of physical and mental debilitation. Then, relief is so strong that the impact of the loss may be softened.

Those friends and relatives who are not quite as close as you are to the dying person may have worked through their anticipatory grief more fully. Occasionally these friends and relatives may underestimate the sharp edge of your grief, thinking that you had worked through all your grief and thereby underestimating the suffering, fright, and loneliness which still remain. You will, hopefully, try to communicate this to them so they can respond lovingly to your real situation, not the one they imagine.

This sense of relief, which is often present after a long illness, can create a problem. You might have twinges of guilt over feeling "good" or "glad" that someone you love has died. You might suppress this sense of relief because you think it is unloving. Actually, the opposite is true; you are relieved because you loved him or her and are glad that the pain and suffering is over. If this guilt gets strong it can short-circuit completion of bereavement grief.

The fact that your experience of anticipatory grief reduces, perhaps significantly, the intensity of bereavement grief may create problems between you and friends or other members of the family. They may expect you to grieve more than you will or think your lack of grief is either inappropriate or means you did not care. You might be tempted to fake more grief than you feel just to make them happy.

I have found that many times those family members who are emotionally close to the dying person but cannot be present continuously during the terminal illness do not work through their anticipatory grief as completely as you will. In fact, they may have used so much denial and held such inappropriate hopes that they have not experienced anticipatory grief at all and, therefore, at the time of death will be plunged into bereavement grief. They will not understand why your grief about the loss is not as intense or deep as theirs and may even accuse you of not loving the deceased as much as they. They may also have trouble accepting the comparative quickness with which you move through your bereavement to a time of acceptance and reaffirmation of life.

I knew one twenty-eight-year-old woman who died slowly of a brain tumor. In the last months she became unable to communicate with or even recognize her husband, finally becoming unconscious during the last weeks. The husband's experience of anticipatory grief was intense over many months. When death finally came, he was relieved as well as sad. His bereavement was less intense than her parents who had denied some of the realities and held unrealistic hopes. After death they went through an intense, long-lasting bereavement grief. When the husband (their son-in-law) remarried just nine months later, they were appalled, thinking of him as disloyal and even suspecting that he had somehow cheated their daughter. This difference in the grief process caused significant disruption in their relationship to their son-in-law and their two grandchildren.

One of my students described how his father had moved through anticipatory grief quite well, while he himself had refused to grieve during his mother's long illness with cancer. Since his grief did not begin until after her death, and even then was delayed at several points, it was difficult for him to accept his father's remarriage a year later. He had not finished grieving, but his father was ready to affirm life and experience resurrection.

In chapter 8 we will talk about the healing of grief.

Notes

1. Phyllis R. Silverman, "Anticipatory Grief from the Perspective of Widowhood," in Bernard Schoenberg, et al., editors, *Anticipatory Grief* (New York: Columbia University Press, 1974), p. 321.

2. *Ibid.*, p. 331.

3. Carl A. Nighswonger, "The Vectors and Vital Signs in Grief Synchronization," in Schoenberg, *op. cit.*, pp. 267-275. See also other articles in this work, such as those by C. Knight Aldrich, pp. 3-9, and Allan W. Reed, pp. 346-357.

4. *Ibid.*, p. 268.

5. Robert B. Reeves, Jr., "Reflections on Two False Expectations," in Schoenberg, *op. cit.*, p. 282.

6. James A. Knight, "Anticipatory Grief," in Austin H. Kutscher, ed., *Death and Bereavement* (Springfield, Ill.: Charles C. Thomas, 1969), pp. 198-199.

7. See Barney G. Glaser and Anselm L. Strauss, *Awareness of Dying* (Chicago: Aldine Publishing Company, 1966).

7
Oh, My God!
(The Crisis of Bereavement Grief)

It is a truth that most of us live as if death were not a reality. We never expect, therefore, that death would intervene in our most meaningful relationships. Death is not only something that happens to the other person, it is also something that happens to the other person's family. We somehow forget the reality that no human escapes this devastating episode in life. It is universal; but there are no explanations, no preparations for the experience. For these reasons, grief hits you hard from the beginning.

When the doctor stepped out the room you could tell by his bowed head and the set look on his face that death had come.

The phone awakened you out of a fitful sleep, and you knew intuitively that the waiting was over.

The door bell rang, and a military chaplain stood on your porch with hat in hand, and your heart stood still.

The frail body in the bed expelled a long breath, and the hand you held went limp.

It was the emergency room nurse saying something about an automobile accident, "He's hurt seriously." You rushed frantically, but you got there too late.

Death happened again, but this time to someone *you* loved. You couldn't believe it! Then the hurt came and the tears, but it's hard to remember everything. The shock and numbness dulls some of it, but some of the pain, anger, and suffering are still excruciatingly clear.

Because we do not know what to expect, the experience of grief is puzzling to us, some of it is frightening and threatening. The emotional and physical effect is disturbing. This experience is probably different from anything you have dealt with before. You may, like many, be so shaken by your thoughts and feelings that you fear losing your mind!

This chapter will introduce you to grief as others have experienced it. We will also seek to understand the dynamics of grief from both the emotional and interpersonal perspectives. I hope you will come to understand that what you experience is not as abnormal as you might think. I believe that understanding the process of grief and the meaning of grief may be of help.

What Is Grief?

The pain and suffering, hurt and fear, anger and guilt, loneliness and despair which closes in on you when death strikes a person you love is *grief.* Any significant loss results in grief; but in this chapter, we are focusing on the most intense loss, that which occurs because of death.

Some have suggested that grief is an unique emotion which in itself represents a different kind of human feeling. Others use the word grief to refer to the complex variety of emotional reactions (normally including anxiety, anger, depression, guilt, and fear) which one has in response to a significant loss. For our purposes, grief is the variety of intense psychological and physiological reactions to the loss of a significant relationship due to the death of a person with whom one was emotionally involved.

The Process of Grief

The impact and meaning of losing a significant person in one's life is unique for each person. It is important for you to remember as you read this chapter that no two individuals experience the anxiety of grief in exactly the same way. However, there are many common aspects to our response to loss. As the experience of grief has been studied, these common aspects have been identified. They form a pattern, or a process, which makes grief more understandable. We have also learned through a growing body of research and observation that moving through all phases of grief is important to reclaiming abundant life. Those who do not move through the whole process are liable to have an aborted grief process which can have negative effects on their future emotional, physical, and spiritual health.

Wayne Oates has given a very inclusive description of this grief process which can serve as an outline for our discussion. He describes six "psychological phases": (1) the shocking blow of the loss, (2) the numbing effect of the shock, (3) the struggle between fantasy and reality, (4) the breakthrough of the flood of grief, (5) selective memory and stabbing pain, and (6) the acceptance of loss and the reaffirmation of life.[1]

Shock. News of an unexpected death triggers a reaction in our bodies and minds called shock. [This reaction reveals the inability of the heart and mind to absorb the reality with which a person is confronted.]The self is simply unable, at first, to digest what has happened.

Our internal reaction is the same as if we had been attacked by some unseen assailant or suffered a physical wound. People express it like this: "It was as if I had been kicked in the stomach." "I felt like cold water had been poured over me." "I thought I would suffocate, I couldn't breathe."

Disbelief crowds the mind. "It can't be, I saw him yesterday." "There must be a mistake!" "No, no, no, it can't be!" The shock may be intense for hours; and, with some reduction in intensity, may last for days or weeks, depending upon many factors. Our emotional defense system attempts to deny what has happened. [Denial is strongest during this phase as our self seeks protection from the frightening, painful reality.]

Numbness. [Nature helps protect us with its own anesthetic.] After the initial shock there is a period of numbness in which the individual feels physically and emotionally paralyzed. It is as if nature stuns our mind and heart to protect it from pain we can't handle. "I can't feel anything." During this phase, thinking, feeling, and moving are all slowed; and the individual appears to have little reaction to the situation. This slowdown and apparent lack of reaction or feeling may trouble the griever and make him or her wonder what's wrong. "I'm just numb all over, I can hardly make myself think." "I can't even cry, what's wrong with me?"

Occasionally observers will misinterpret this phase and conclude that the individual is not experiencing any grief. When people are saying, "How well she is holding up," or "He is taking it so well," they do not realize that the grief-stricken person is still in the shock and numbness phases of their reaction. These same people are then surprised when strong emotions are expressed at later times.

Gradually, the numbness wears off, and the person experiences any or all of the next three phases.

Fantasy Versus Reality. It is difficult for the self to accept the reality of the loss and "let go" of the deceased individual. Your mind conjures up fantasies that momentarily make you feel he or she is present. You might think you see him on the street, hear her come in the front door, or hear his voice calling from another room. Occasionally the dreams are so realistic that you are convinced for minutes that the loved person is still alive. These fantasies and hallucinations often contribute to the feeling that you might be "losing your mind" or "cracking up."

Psychologically we move ahead *as if* he or she were still present. One widow in a church I served talked about how she caught herself serving two places for dinner before being jarred back into the painful reality that her husband would not be coming in for dinner. One seminarian shared that there was a car on the seminary campus just like the one his mother drove. He described his inability to keep from looking at the driver each time the car passed to see if it were his mother, even though she had died months earlier.

Flood of Grief. During the weeks and months following death, particularly after one of the fantasies mentioned above, the reality of the loss will cut through our numbness, slice through our surface adjustments, and trigger a flood of hurt expressed usually through strong weeping. It is disturbing to some grievers because this flood of grief seems to be out of control. This is the way our self deals with the pain of its loss. This flood of grief can have a very cathartic and cleansing effect on us after it is over. Because of the taboos in our society related to males crying, many men have difficulty with this stage of grief. Often they will be embarrassed to do this weeping in front of other people or to allow other people to know it occurs.

Those people who choke back these tears, maintain spartan control over crying, and resist it because they think it is a testimony to lack of faith will almost certainly be negatively affected by these unexpressed tears sometime in the future.

Selective Memory and Stabbing Pain.   As the weeks and months go by, the vivid fantasies subside and less intense memories and associations become more dominant. A song, a place, a person, a scrapbook, a picture will recall events and happenings from the past. These memories rekindle the pain of the loss, not as acutely as the fantasies, but with sharp thrusts that can still be upsetting and spark periods of crying. These memories are more related to the realities of the past than to the unrealities of the present and are not usually as frightening.

Acceptance of Loss and Reaffirmation of Life.   This final phase of grief may begin within days of the loss or may not start for many months, depending on the intensity of the grief and other circumstances. It will then take many weeks, months, and even years to complete. Oates describes this phase beautifully:

From a psychological point of view, the individual himself undergoes a death, burial, and resurrection of his selfhood in the process of grief, first rejecting life in the face of death and then accepting death in the face of life. In the losing of life, life itself is gained.[2]

We will discuss more about the process of healing grief in the next chapter, but first we must elaborate on some other aspects of the grief process.

Grief and Your Body

Grief affects you physically in two ways. First, the initial phases of grief include many physical symptoms and sensations. Secondly, in the later stages of grief real health problems can occur.

One of the major surprises of the grief experience is the physical distress which accompanies this anxiety. Grief anxiety is almost always accompanied by a physical reaction related to the operation of the central nervous system.[3] The bereaved persons with whom Lindemann worked, for example, reported:

> Sensations of [physical] distress occurring in waves lasting from twenty minutes to an hour at a time, a feeling of tightness in the throat, choking with shortness of breath, need for sighing, an empty feeling in the abdomen, lack of muscular power, and an intensive subjective distress described as tension or mental pain.[4]

Bereaved people breathe unevenly and more slowly than usual. They occasionally sigh deeply or gasp as if breathing was a laborious task. Sometimes there is a feeling of suffocation.

A lack of strength and a feeling of exhaustion make the bereaved feel that every action demands effort. Bernadine Kreis reported "a constant internal quivering" that made her legs extremely weak and made it difficult at times to walk or even stand erect.[5] Others say: "It is all I can do to climb the stairs." "I can hardly lift anything, I'm so weak." "Doing anything makes me exhausted!"

Eating problems are also common. Food is tasteless and sticks in one's throat, swallowing is difficult, indigestion occurs, the stomach feels hollow, little or no appetite is present, often resulting in a loss of weight.

Other physical complaints include a tightness in the chest which makes people feel that there is a "weight on it," trembling, fainting, dizziness, and insomnia. Other bereaved people report symptoms and feelings such as general nervousness, feelings of fear or panic, irritability, restlessness, nightmares, fatigue, and being "on edge." You may have noticed in your own grief similar symptoms and perhaps some that were unique to you.

Grief is so disturbing to a person's total adjustment that it may lead to serious health problems in the later stages. For example, one way that grief affects your health is by reducing your overall resistance so you are more vulnerable to real diseases and illnesses.

Studies like those cited by Parks [6] show bereaved individuals have a higher incidence of physical illness in the first year after the death event than they did in the prior year and also higher than that for control groups of nonbereaved persons. Grieved people themselves report their health is worse during the first twelve to eighteen months of bereavement. Several studies show that visits to doctors and the incidence of hospitalization is increased for widows and widowers in the period of time following the death event.[7] To what degree illnesses are psychological in origin is hard to determine but certainly the emotional impact of grief is a major factor. Some bereaved people have experienced significant increase in the intensity and severity of illnesses which they had already experienced, such as colitis, asthma, arthritis, and rheumatism.[8]

A second way in which grief affects health is that many bereaved persons find themselves plagued by symptoms of the illness which killed their loved one.[9] One student talked at length about the heart pains which he experienced in the months after his father died of a heart attack. These symptoms, of course, are unrelated to any real disease entity and are identified as psychogenic. Still they are very real to the bereaved and increases the overall anxiety of grief.

Loneliness and Despondency

One of the heaviest feelings in a time of bereavement is the feeling of loneliness. After sharing a significant part of our emotional and physical life with another person, we get used to having them with us. We depend on their conversation, their support, and all interactions which we shared. When taken out of our lives it creates a huge void. For those losing a spouse there is an immediate loss of sexual satisfaction and all of the meaning which this can contribute to one's life. One of my professional colleagues, while describing to a class of seminarians his grief over his wife's death, expressed it like this:

After Mother had gone home, acute loneliness and a deep feeling of personal deprivation began to seep into the crevices of my consciousness and penetrate out to my fingertips. One of the most horrible feelings I think a human being can have is to know the nature of, and to have the experience of, an extremely intimate marital relationship—to love a person more than one loves his own body, then to realize without any apparent reason . . . that this wonderful, warm, and affectionate person is gone.

In this horrifying loneliness, which is the most empty and depressing sensation that I have ever experienced in my life, one begins to become aware of what it means to be so physically and emotionally deprived of the person that one loves, that every nerve-ending in the body seems to cry out for contact with that individual. You don't feel it in your mind, it's all over your whole body.

This feeling of deprivation and loneliness, this sensation of being so emotionally torn apart, is such that one feels like he's got either a great big rock in his chest or that a hole has been carved out and part of his own flesh has been pulled away from him.

It is this extreme sense of loneliness that leads to despondency and even despair. You can feel so low, sad, and unhappy. The emptiness is difficult to bear. The emotional suffering can become so intense that you may have thought you would die. For some it seems so unbearable that they wish they could die and, of course, in some instances grieved persons have indeed taken their own lives or grieved themselves to death.

It may be this sense of loss and loneliness which makes the bereaved feel so vulnerable and so fearful. Many grievers report how much their grief seems like an experience of fear. You may have, in your own grief, had an indescribable and unspecific dread of the future or worried that something tragic was going to occur again.

Why Grief?

How could the death of any person cause so much anguish, so many intense responses, over such a long period of time? You may have raised such a question when you look back on the early stages of your grief. Our common sense lets us know that to love someone and to lose them is to suffer, and for some that is enough to know. But perhaps you would like to understand it more deeply.

David Switzer, a minister and a psychologist, has contributed significantly to our understanding of why we grieve. In his book

The Dynamics of Grief he takes the position that grief is basically related to anxiety. He states: "Grief has as its core experience an acute attack of anxiety, precipitated by . . . the death of a person with whom one is emotionally involved." [10] He does not deny that grief is characterized by many other feelings (such as guilt, depression, sadness, fear, and anger) but thinks that "all of the behavioral responses observed and reported in grief are in some way related to this anxiety." [11] Anxiety can be described as our emotional and physical response to anything which threatens our self, our personhood, our existence.

Where does this anxiety come from? One source is the experience of separation from significant people (like parents) during infancy and childhood leading to a phenomenon psychologists call "separation anxiety." [12] As infants we were very dependent on mothering persons to meet our needs. Adults took care of hunger, messiness, and acutal pain. We learned that the presence of a caring person meant that our needs were met and a sense of well-being, fulfillment, and happiness prevailed. Infants and children learn that the absence of a caring person might mean their needs will go unmet and they will be unloved.

As we grew older we learned that being needed by others and meeting their needs was a way of feeling complete and worthwhile. Most of us grew into adulthood deeply dependent on interpersonal relationships for a sense of well-being and "at easeness" in our existence. We work hard at establishing and keeping meaningful relationships, and when we are separated from them (such as when one leaves school, joins the military, moves to another city, gets married, gets divorced) anxiety results. Death, of course, is the most final of separations and therefore creates the most intense separation anxiety.

John Bowlby has shown that children who are separated from their mothers and adults who have suffered separation by death react with the similar responses of fear, despair, withdrawal, confusion, a sense of emptiness, lack of motivation, reduced activity, hostility, and guilt. [13]

Another source of the anxiety which underlies grief is related to our fear of death, the feeling of responsibility we have for our lives, and questions about the meaning of life. These three concerns relate to our basic existence as human beings and can be referred to by the term "existential anxiety." [14] Three aspects of this existential anxiety intrude into the experience of grief: (1) the fear of our own death, (2) questioning the meaning of life, and (3) the reality of our limitations as human beings.

Since death is an unknown, we usually have some apprehension about what it is like. It is scary, cold, final, painful. Even those whose religious faith teaches that death is not the end are influenced by the cultural attitude toward death characterized by fear and anxiety and are consequently anxious about their own death. How does this affect grief? Well, most of us are not able to imagine our own death, but when death claims a loved one we are impressed with its realness. Death's undisclosed secrets are frightening; and our own fears about death, which are normally suppressed, surface in the form of grief anxiety.

Grief includes the questioning of life's meaning because we invest so much of our hope in life in those interpersonal relationships within which we have invested ourselves. When death breaks one of these significant relationships, through which we have identified and defined so much of our lives, then we wonder what life is about. Is it fate which rules? Could it be blind chance or some unplanned chaos? The question "Why?" asked by every bereaved person reveals the underlying uncertainty, "If this person in whom I have invested so much and loved so dearly dies, what happens to the meaning of our relationship? And if that meaning is gone, can any part of life be meaningful?"

Death also reminds us of our finitude, that is the limitations of being human, made of flesh, subject to time and space, vulnerable to pain and disease. How helpless we are in the face of illness, accident, war, irresponsibility, and the resulting death. Our anxiousness in the face of this helplessness and our vulnerability to the unknown contributes to the anxiety of grief.

Guilt and Anger

As indicated at several points already, the experience of bereavement is often accompanied by feelings of guilt and hostility, to the surprise of many bereaved individuals. Why this guilt and hostility?

One reason is related to the feeling of responsibility for our lives and the events which take place in our lives. Paul Tillich refers to this phenomenon as the "anxiety of guilt and condemnation." [15] When death strikes, many people feel that the tragedy somehow results from their irresponsibility. Somehow they feel that they are to blame ("What did I do wrong?"). It is as if we could deny our human limitations if we could demonstrate that the death was related to human cause. Mrs. Kreis, when sharing the feelings of guilt she experienced in her grief, later realized that her guilt reflected her irrational feelings that she "should have been powerful enough to save my husband's life!" [16]

Hostile feelings can also be an expression of this frustration over our human limitations and our attempt to fight against our helplessness. Often the hostility of the bereaved person strikes out in all directions as if in some way a fight could be picked with fate.

The guilt and hostility which accompany grief have some of their origins in the same emotional history as does separation anxiety. [17] As we said, children learn early of their dependence on caring persons. They also learn how to maintain the love and approval of these caring persons by shaping their behavior according to the parents' wishes and requirements. As adults we often do the same; we strive to keep the approval of those on whom we are dependent, those upon whom we depend for meaning, by adjusting our behavior and our lives to our perceptions of what they want us to be. Many parents in our culture punish children by threatening to withhold love and affection. Children learn to fear that doing something the caring people don't like will cause them to leave or withdraw (separation anxiety).

We often maintain this same stance and carry this same fear into adulthood. Consequently, when a loved one dies our unconscious mind may feel they have "separated" from us because we had done something wrong, hence the feeling of self-blame and responsibility for their death. We may assume, unconsciously, that the separation would not have occurred had we not done something wrong or something which the deceased disapproved.[18]

Immediately after the death the grief-stricken survivor may blame himself or herself because of a particular event, word, deed, or oversight. ("If only we hadn't let them operate!" "I should have called the doctor sooner!") The questions asked doctors, witnesses, and other relatives often reflect the concern over finding cause or reason for the death, particularly with reference to ascertaining responsibility. ("Was there anything I could have done?")

Realistically we must accept that some guilt accompanying grief is real guilt and related to real failure in our relationship with the deceased person or of actual irresponsibility with reference to the death. For example, the young father of a little girl who was killed in a one-car accident in which he was the driver had to face the fact that his careless driving while drinking contributed to the death of his daughter. His experience of guilt was real; and before his grief could heal he had to confess this guilt, accept God's forgiveness, and forgive himself.

Hostility directed at other people or institutions is often the other side of this coin. Anger can be the bereaved's attempt to locate blame and responsibility outside of himself or herself. Self-blame is painful; so to perceive that the death was facilitated by the doctors, the hospital, the mechanic who worked on the plane before takeoff, the relative who lived with them, the friend who was driving, or even God can be an attempt to protect against these feelings of guilt.

We must also accept that some hostility is appropriate and realistic. Sometimes death would not have occurred if it weren't for such things as pilot error, drunk drivers, icy streets, misdiagnoses, armed robbers, and irresponsibility on the part of the deceased.

Sometimes the blame is located on the deceased and the hostility focused in that direction. ("He always drove too fast!" "I could never get her to a doctor, now look what has happened!") In reality, of course, humans do contribute to their own death, they drive too fast and hide symptoms from doctors until the disease has progressed too far. Making distinctions between the reality and the fantasy √ concerning these feelings is part of the healing of grief.

Separation anxiety also gets focused on the deceased, resulting in a great deal of hostility. ("How could she have left me with three children to care for?" "How could he leave me when our business is so far in debt?")

Separation anxiety surfaces as guilt more clearly if death has been by suicide. The survivor usually feels that he or she contributed to the death and wonders if other people are thinking the same thing. Guilt is also experienced when the bereaved person feels relieved that death has finally occurred after a long terminal illness or when advanced age had taken a heavy emotional and physical toll.

Human relationships, even the best, have both negative and positive aspects. At death the bereaved may blame himself or herself for the negative aspects of the relationship. ("I shouldn't have nagged him so often about making more money." "We fought over the kids all the time even though I knew her ideas were correct." "If I could only have trusted him more.") Some hostility is also directed at the deceased for their part in the negative aspects of the relationship. Such ambivalence is to be anticipated, and the bereaved should not feel abnormal when experiencing mixtures of positive and negative feelings. These positive and negative feelings are often expressed through dreams which can be quite disturbing.

One last word about anger and guilt. You may feel angry at God for not preventing the death. If he is all-powerful, why didn't he make the cars miss each other, eradicate the cancer, dissolve the blockage in the artery, or prevent the child from getting near the water? You may have shaken your fist at God for allowing so much suffering. Questioning God's love and doubting that he cares for you often go hand-in-hand with grief. If you experience this anger toward God, you may also feel guilty for daring to feel angry at the Creator, thinking that it is inappropriate or ungrateful.

Coming to grips with these guilty and hostile feelings are part of the healing of grief which will be discussed in the following chapter.

Notes

1. Wayne E. Oates, *Anxiety in Christian Experience* (Philadelphia: The Westminster Press, 1955), pp. 51-56.

2. *Ibid.*, pp. 54-55.

3. George Engel, "Is Grief a Disease?" *Psychosomatic Medicine,* XXIII (1961), pp. 18-22.

4. Erich Lindemann, "Symptomatology and Management of Acute Grief," *Pastoral Psychology,* XIV (1963).

5. Bernadine Kreis and Alice Pattie, *Up from Grief: Patterns of Recovery* (New York: The Seabury Press, 1969), p. 21.

6. Colin Murray Parkes, *Bereavement: Studies of Grief in Adult Life* (New York: International Universities Press, Inc., 1972), pp. 14-28.

7. *Ibid.*

8. *Ibid.*

9. David K. Switzer, *The Dynamics of Grief: Its Source, Pain, and Healing* (Nashville: Abingdon Press, 1970), pp. 113-114.

10. *Ibid.*, pp. 12-13.

11. *Ibid.*, p. 93.

12. See Switzer, *The Dynamics of Grief,* chapter 4.

13. John Bowlby, "Grief and Mourning in Early Infancy and Childhood," *The Psychoanalytic Study of the Child,* XV (1960), pp. 17-20.

14. See Switzer, *The Dynamics of Grief,* chapter 6.

15. Paul Tillich, *The Courage to Be* (New Haven, Conn.: Yale University Press, 1952), pp. 51-54.

16. Kreis and Pattie, *Up from Grief,* p. 17.

17. Switzer, *The Dynamics of Grief,* p. 119.

18. See Parkes, *Bereavement,* chapter 6; gives many examples of this experience.

8
Wiping Away the Tears
(Recovering from Grief)

We have now described your encounter with acute bereavement and/or your involvement with anticipatory grief. What then shall we say about your response as a Christian to these experiences? We know that the trauma of these events has been physically, emotionally, and spiritually difficult for you, perhaps even devastating. Your life has been significantly affected, and you have many questions and concerns.

Now what? When our physical bodies are seriously wounded, we must allow them to heal before resuming an active life. It is equally true of the emotional/spiritual wound caused by a significant loss or the threat of such a loss. You will not be able to pursue again an abundant life until this wound can heal. What do we know from those who have studied and experienced grief that could help you in your pilgrimage through this crisis? What resources are available through our Christian faith? We will suggest some answers after responding to a question you may have asked.

Should the Christian Grieve?

Some Christians wonder if it is a sign of weak faith to grieve when a loved one dies. They ask, "If we believe he or she has gone to be with God, shouldn't we be celebrating instead of mourning?" This is a good question, for certainly we believe our dead loved ones are in some way still within God's care and within his providence. Certainly we believe they have received the gift of eternal life and that we will meet them again at the resurrection, so why not be happy instead of sad? That sounds good; but what are we to make of this unquestionable emotional pain, this heartache, this anxiety created in us by the loss? Is it possible to believe positive and feel negative at the same time? I think so.

Some would suggest that Christians should not grieve, because they think Christians should never have strong negative feelings of any kind. They assume that having faith in God keeps us from experiencing sadness, anxiety, disappointment, fear, anger, doubt, or, of course, grief which may include all of these. From my perspective, these Christians want to let their faith raise them above real human life, or at least protect them from it.

My belief is different. I believe that our Christian faith enables us to creatively encounter our human existence rather than protecting us from it. To be human is to be limited by time and space. We are vulnerable to pain, suffering, illness, separation, and death! We have been created with the potential for feeling emotions such as joy, love, anger, and grief in response to our human situation. To deny this part of ourselves is to deny the nature of God's creation.

Jesus was not only fully God but was fully human, and he provides us with a model for experiencing our full humanness. Since the Gospels portray Jesus as a person who felt a wide range of emotions, we can believe that emotions are also part of our humanness. "Jesus wept" as he spoke to Mary and her friends about the death of Lazarus, her brother (John 11:33-35), and when coming to the tomb was "deeply moved again" (John 11:38). Can we feel any less when one we loved dies?

Participating in the pain and suffering of grief is one of the ways we experience our humanity and are confronted with the limitations of our finiteness. Another reason we as Christians experience grief is our commitment to love. We believe love is central to the Christian gospel. Jesus clearly stated that the greatest commandment is to "love the Lord your God" and "love your neighbor as yourself" (Mark 12:28-31). We are committed to giving ourselves in love to other people as God has lovingly given himself to us.

Loving others means to invest ourselves in them, intertwine our lives with theirs, and share intimately their concerns. In doing this we make ourselves vulnerable to emotional pain and grief. When

Jesus wept about Lazarus the people said, "Behold how he loved him!" (John 11:36). After experiencing a significant, love-filled, marital relationship to the depths of warmth and intimacy possible in God's creation, it would be impossible not to suffer when that relationship was broken by death. As my colleague, whom I have quoted in the previous chapter, said about his relationship to his deceased wife:

I have come to realize through personal experience that when you talk of love you are talking about pain, about deprivation. If you don't want to suffer, don't ever let yourself love. The more you love the more you are going to hurt. [I know now that] the commitment of oneself, the exposure of one's being, the relating of oneself to another person in a loving relationship is worth all the pain that you might have to endure because of the loss.

When the Christians at Thessalonica were concerned about the future of their dead loved ones, Paul wrote to assure them that they did not have to "grieve as others do who have no hope" (1 Thess. 4:13). Paul said, "We believe that Jesus died and rose again," and that when he comes again, "God will bring with him those who have fallen asleep" (4:14). Since these early Christians believed without question that Jesus was going to return any day and since they therefore assumed they would be reunited with their loved ones at any moment, Paul may have been indicating that they did not have to grieve at all.

Those of us in this age, however, know that Jesus Christ did not return immediately, nor has he come in the intervening years. Most of us assume, therefore, that much time will pass before we are reunited with our loved ones. I think if Paul were writing a letter to us today, speaking to our concerns about grief, he might well use the same words. However, I do not think his words would emphasize "it is not necessary to grieve because your loved ones will return soon" but would emphasize "yes you grieve, but let your grief be different than those who do not believe."

How? Those who do not believe in resurrection and eternal life grieve as if there were no future, as if all personal existence had come to an end. They grieve in despair over life's lack of meaning. As Christians we grieve over our present losses and admit the suffering death creates in our lives, but from a different perspective. Our experience with God as he revealed himself in the life, death, and resurrection of Jesus Christ tempers our grief with faith that the creation has ultimate meaning, with hope in resurrection, with assurance of eternal life, and with trust in the steadfast love of God.

The Need for Communication With People

Of crucial importance in the healing of grief is the need to communicate what you are experiencing to other human beings. Conversation, hours and hours of talking, will be the major vehicle through which you can accomplish the healing of your grief.

Talking is the most significant way in which you and I as human beings express ourselves. Of course, we communicate ourselves through our bodies and through our nonverbal actions; but primarily humans use words. Putting words to your grief enables you to share it with another person.

Indeed this is another reason for the importance of communication; it means you are relating to other people. Most of us depend on our community of family, friends, neighbors, and fellow Christians for support and understanding. In a time of crisis their importance to us multiplies, and to depend on them at this point in time is quite appropriate. Within this community of people, God will be ministering to you. He will be loving you through their caring, understanding you through their empathy, granting grace through their concern.

The importance of relating to other people, of talking about our grief, and experiencing God within this communication with others was expressed quite well by my colleague in a sharing session after his wife died.

I suppose that if I had not had a family that cared—a Christian community who expressed the love of God in both invisible and tangible ways, and two individuals who shared their love with deep concern and compassion, I might have actually collapsed completely. . . . I have come to the conclusion for myself that I don't have any strength nor any power as a solitary individual. For me the representatives of God's grace have been my sons, my pastor, my colleagues, and these two very, very dear friends with whom I have spent hours in personal conversation either on the telephone or sitting together at home or somewhere over a cup of coffee talking, talking, talking, talking for hours without end, about the experience, about the deprivation, about the longing, about the problems of re-adjustment, about every conceivable interest and concern that has been affected by this experience of death and grief.

For you to find people with whom you can share yourself this openly and completely will not be easy. Some members of your family and some friends will not want you to talk freely about your grief because it makes them uncomfortable. As we have said before, some people are afraid of deep emotions; and therefore they will worry that you will become emotional, "break down," or "go to pieces." They won't know what to do with your tears and your agony. They will feel helpless in front of your needs and your anguish. So they will encourage you to talk about other things, suggest that you "forget it now," and rush you toward normal living much too quickly. Our society expects people to "get over it" in a hurry and underestimates the amount of time which it takes to recover from a significant grief experience.

However, if you are willing to try, you can find friends and relatives who will be more sensitive, more patient, and less threatened. Those who have suffered through a grief of their own will be more likely to empathize with your experience and recognize the importance of conversation. Many pastors are trained to listen and respond creatively to persons in crises.

Prayer could be a significant resource to you in your grief. Prayer can be defined as our total communication with God. At its best prayer can be a time of deep, personal sharing of our concerns with our Father in heaven. Although the early shock, numbness, and disbelief in grief can blunt your communication with God, it will not be long before you will be able to disclose your innermost thoughts and feelings to him. Even when you find it difficult to express yourself remember: "Likewise the Spirit helps us in our weakness; for we do not know how to pray as we ought, but the Spirit himself intercedes for us with sighs too deep for words" (Rom. 8:26).

Accepting the Reality of Death

Perhaps the necessary first step in the healing of grief is accepting the reality of the death which has occurred. Many factors work against your acceptance. Our society's fear of death, and its resultant attempt to deny and hide from it, affects us all. Death takes place hidden in intensive care units of hospitals, in old-age homes, or on highways, not at home. Our funeral practices portray sleep, not death. Our own denial makes us disbelieve this death could happen, but it has; and recognition of death's reality is necessary to working through the anxiety of grief.

Death is universal, everyone will die. Your loved one is dead and no longer available to you in this life. We must remember that the Christian gospel is not afraid of death, even though it identifies death as an enemy (1 Cor. 15:26). Death is a reality of human existence. Even Jesus Christ, the Son of God, died a real death. How could he be resurrected if he had not allowed himself to experience the reality of death? The gospel does not proclaim that God protects us from death, but that he brings life out of death through resurrection.

Facing and Expressing Your Grief

Wayne Oates has pointed out that one of the theological truths about grief is the importance of accepting "the Way of the Cross." [1] That is, suffering is an integral part of life which marks our humanity and must be accepted and faced if our existence is to be completely human. It is tempting to hide from the suffering related to grief instead of facing it and overcoming it.

People will suggest that you dodge the suffering of grief by saying, "put it out of your mind," or, "don't think about it." Their intentions are good, but unrealistic and not the way of Christian faith. Blocking out grief can contribute to emotional and spiritual illness.

Thinking about your grief is necessary even though painful. You will probably need, for example, to reflect on the death itself. What caused the death? What were the events surrounding the death? Was any particular person responsible? Could anything have been done to prevent it? These and many other questions need to be dealt with openly and honestly. Some of them will have answers and some will not. But it is important to deal with them so that, when you close the door on this particular chapter of your life, there will be no poisons to affect you at a later time.

Facing the memories can be saddening, but memories can be one of life's treasures and to lose them would be tragic. Recovering from grief does not mean erasing all memories of the dead person and your relationship with him or her. Indeed, the most complete healing can take place when you can look at pictures, hear the music, visit the familiar places, handle the favorite toys, wear the last present, and in other ways accept memories as part of the celebration and thanksgiving for having lived a portion of life with this person whom you loved so much. In living with the memories, instead of running from them, the pain diminishes and appreciation for what the person gave to you and accepted from you will increase.

Expressing the emotions of grief is also important. Weeping is a very normal and healthy reaction to grief. Some people will say things like: "Don't break down; it will upset your children." "There's no use crying, it won't bring your husband back." "Buck up, son, be a man now and don't cry." But keeping back this weeping would be a mistake. Tuck quotes an old Chinese proverb that says, "If you do not weep outwardly, you will weep inwardly." [2] Psychologists have learned how true this is, for grief unexpressed can cause emotional and physical problems in the future. "The deep ache, sore hurt, and bottled-up feelings need to be expressed, and no mourner need feel any sense of apology or disgrace for weeping." [3] If it frightens or threatens others for you to weep, don't hold back. Excuse yourself and find a corner where you can be alone or with relatives and friends who are able to understand and cry until you feel relieved.

Jesus did not mind weeping at the tomb of his friend Lazarus. Your ability to cry is nature's safety valve for your intense emotions. To cap this safety valve may cause a later explosion.

Reconciling Negative Emotions

We have already described how guilt and anger play a part in the grief experience. It is important in the healing of grief for you to admit to yourself the extent and intensity of these feelings. When you can admit them to yourself, then share them with a trusted person so that you can move toward accepting these feelings and deal with them appropriately and realistically. Talking out these feelings is one way of releasing the stored-up energy invested in these emotions.

Reaction of friends and relatives to expressions of guilt will often be hasty reassurances that your guilt is unfounded and absurd. This reassurance might inhibit your need to talk it out and decide for yourself if some guilt is real. You will want to face openly and honestly any part of your guilt that seems to be real, so that you can confess that guilt and ask forgiveness concerning it.

When faced with any expressed hostility toward the deceased, some of these same people will be shocked and think you unfair, unappreciative, or without respect for the dead. Again, this response might keep you from fully expressing and examining these angry emotions. It is important for you to find some perceptive and sensitive person who will help you explore which of these feelings is based on reality and which are not. Ascertaining the difference will help you accept those which are part of the fantasy of grief and those which are based on reality and take responsibility for expressing them in appropriate directions. Only when these negative feelings of guilt and hostility are dealt with appropriately, can you expect to experience reconciliation in the healing process.

Breaking the Ties that Bind

Part of your grief relates to the significant investment of yourself and your life in the person now dead. You had shared so much, directed a great deal of energy in their direction, and included them in your plans, dreams, and reasons for existence. Now they are gone, and you must recognize that emotional investment in a person who has died cannot lead to an abundant life. Slowly but surely you must withdraw from him or her this emotional energy as you would savings from a bank, so that this emotional energy is available to invest in other persons and relationships. Those who cannot "let go" and withdraw this energy become guilty of idolatry. Oates describes this "temptation to idolatry" as the investment of a person in someone who has died to the point that they are unable to recognize the change in reality brought about by that person's death. Instead, they organize and structure their life around a dead person by continuing to focus attention on the death event.[4]

Parents who maintain a child's room in the same state as it was on the day of the child's death is an example of this idolatry. They make a shrine of the room and worship there each day as they idealize the child and unconsciously assume the child will return. It is as if they were frozen in time, and they function as if their child were only asleep in a golden glass casket such as the seven dwarfs made for Snow White. They live as if the child might at any time be awakened by a kiss and resume living as if nothing had happened.

Another illustration of idolatry is the spouse who pledges never to marry again after the death of the husband or wife. Certainly many spouses feel this way in the first months after the death of their spouse. But those who do not remarry because they continue to be concerned that remarriage will "violate the memory" of their first marriage or, believe no one could ever take the place of their former spouse, have raised the dead spouse into position as an idol.

Resurrection of the Dead Within Your Self

Part of you may resist "letting go" or "giving up" the person who has died. It may seem like a cruel or disloyal stance after years of being so close. The persistent feeling that you cannot live without him or her also contributes to the hesitancy to accept the death. It is not necessary, however, to try and forget completely this significant person. Both Oates and Switzer have called attention to the importance of resurrecting the dead person within the life of the bereaved.[5]

This resurrection involves incorporating the personal characteristics and qualities of the deceased into your own selfhood. It is a conscious integration of certain aspects of his or her life energy, values, commitments, fulfillments, goals, and purposes, into your own personality so they become part of your life.

This is not the same thing as imagining that the dead person has taken over your life or in some way resides in your body and sits at the controls. That type of identification, if lasting very long, would be a sign of unhealthy grief.

Establishing New Relationships

Bereaved persons who have experienced a full return to abundant life say that a significant ingredient in the healing of grief is the establishment of new relationships. The loneliness of grief is so strong, the feeling of loss and emptiness so great, that only real, live people can fill the void. We are interpersonal creatures, and the need for relationships is one of our strongest human needs. It was probably difficult for you to relate during the early weeks of grief, and I know you are grateful for those sensitive people who continued to take initiative toward you. But the time comes when you must reach out, fighting through the withdrawal and depression, to reestablish relationships with people who have been important to you in the past and establish new relationships with people you have never known before.

Switzer points out that one meaning of love in the Christian faith is "union."[6] Since grief represents our intense response to separation, we can appreciate how much death threatens our feelings about loving and being loved. When you reestablish old relationships and begin seeking intimacy with other persons, you are generating new love and bringing about union between you and other humans. Loving and being loved again, you will be able to overcome the separation and loneliness which is such a heavy part of most grief.

Self-Affirmation

In the midst of intense grief, particularly when mixed with strong feelings of separation anxiety and fear of the future, it is easy for you to question your personal worth. This is particularly true during times of depression and loneliness. During grief you may raise many questions about your behavior, thoughts, and feelings. You might wish you had done some things differently, held your tongue at a certain point, and wonder what others are thinking about you. All this, along with those waves of anger and guilt, may contribute to a loss of self-esteem.

Reestablishing positive attitudes toward yourself is important. You are a person under God who has a life to live, talents to share, and love to give. You will need to listen and believe the affirming things that will be said to you by those who surround you and were said by the one who has died. Your healing will not be complete without reaffirmation of yourself as a person of worth to God and other people.

Discovering New Meaning in Life

We mentioned earlier that the last stage in the process of grief is the rediscovery of meaning. As the other phases of grief are experienced and the healing process moves toward completion, the bereaved can begin to sense again that life has meaning. Loss of a loved one by death does make us question the meaningfulness of life. We know that it is important for humans to have meaning in their lives in order to experience happiness and fulfillment. I hope you can move toward rediscovering meaning in this life, even though it no longer includes a person who was very significant to you.

Your Christian faith can serve as a basic resource in reclaiming purpose and meaning in your life. Our faith affirms that the relationships we have in this life are meaningful and that Jesus has prepared a place for us that will include a reunion at some higher, deeper, more intimate level with those we have loved here.

Yet, our faith also persuades us that meaning in life must transcend human relationships. Our existence must be for purposes that go beyond any one relationship. What specific purposes you may be called to fulfill, I do not know. I hope it will become obvious to you as the months go by. But of one thing we can be assured, that your mission, and mine, are bound up in the commandment to love the Lord our God with all that we are and to love our neighbors as ourselves (Mark 12:29-31).

Notes

1. Wayne E. Oates, *Anxiety in Christian Experience* (Philadelphia: The Westminster Press, 1955). p. 59.

2. William P. Tuck, *Facing Grief and Death* (Nashville: Broadman Press, 1975), p. 37.

3. *Ibid.*

4. Oates, p. 60.

5. Oates, p. 55, and David K. Switzer, *The Dynamics of Grief: Its Source, Pain and Healing* (Nashville: Abingdon Press, 1970), pp. 200-201.

6. Switzer, p. 202.

9
Breaking Up
(The Crisis of Separation and Divorce)

Divorce seems to have reached epidemic proportions in our society. We begin to wonder if the predictions of the sociologists were correct and the nuclear family is dying. Few, if any, people are not affected by divorce which has occurred for a member of their family or good friends. If you are reading this chapter, you may yourself be experiencing a separation or already be divorced. You know the trauma up close and probably agree with Joseph Epstein that "divorce is often necessary yet is seldom accomplished without sadness, pain, and significant loss." [1]

Paul Bohannan has described six aspects of the personal experience of separation and divorce which you are either going through or have been through. [2] First is the "emotional divorce" which centers around the marital conflict leading toward divorce. This period is characterized by increasing separation and alienation within the emotional union of the marriage. Feelings are withheld (and occasionally exploded), but basically the partners are drifting or pulling apart at all emotional levels.

The second "station," as Bohannon calls it, is the "legal divorce." In America, marriage is a legal contract and must be terminated in court before either partner has the right to remarry. The legal separation may also include the next two phases.

The third phase is the "economic divorce" in which the couple must divide up the material possessions which they legally own as if they were one entity. Many of the emotional difficulties between partners may surface during this phase.

The fourth phase is the "coparental divorce" which involves all the decisions about caring for the children. Where should they live?

With whom? What are the visiting privileges? How can each parent relate creatively to the children as an unmarried person?

The "community divorce" is the fifth stage and refers to the vast impact that the divorce will have on family, friends, social groups, and each spouse's place and role in the community.

Lastly comes the stage of "psychic divorce" during which each partner must struggle to achieve individual autonomy. We do become dependent on marriage partners and live in tandem with them. Upon separation it is a significant task to establish a sense of individuality and independence. We will describe some of the emotional dynamics which permeate all these phases of separation and divorce.

Emotional Responses to Divorce

Divorce usually follows a period of marital conflict which is characterized by strong emotional involvement. The separation and divorce usually intensifies these emotions and adds others. The emotional impact affects both spouses, the children, the parents of the partners, and close friends. Some of the more prominent emotional struggles are discussed below.

Grief

As you go through the process of divorce, you will probably be surprised by the amount of grief you feel over the separation. Grief is not one of the emotional responses with which most divorcees expect to contend. This reaction, however, is almost universal in divorce situations. It is also true that both spouses usually experience this feeling of loss, regardless of whether the divorce was mutually agreed upon or initiated and pushed through by one spouse against the will of the other.

Why this grief? As we point out often in this book, our lives are significantly wrapped up with the people to whom we relate intimately. When we suffer a significant loss in our lives, we experience a type of anxiety we call grief. Since people are usually the most important part of our lives, the loss by death or separation usually provokes the strongest experiences of grief. Your spouse was one of the major components in your life, and losing that relationship leaves an emotional vacuum.

Your marriage partner was an individual with whom you have been deeply involved, even if a portion of that involvement has been conflictual and unfulfilling. Like it or not, your identities have been interwoven, you have spent much time together, and you have shared with each other many experiences, both good and bad. To some extent, meaning in your life has come from the relationship which existed between the two of you. During some portion of the time you were married, you considered yourselves to be in love; some of you may still feel that way.

If you are the spouse who has not wanted the divorce, has been pleased with the marriage, and still feel in love with your partner, then the separation or divorce has probably created stronger grief for you than for your partner. You feel a more significant loss because your investment in your spouse and your dependency on the relationship are greater.

If you are the spouse who has taken initiative in the separation or divorce, however, or a partner in a separation or divorce which was agreed upon mutually, you may be surprised to find yourself experiencing grief at all. Since you have been disengaging for awhile, withdrawing some of the emotional investment from this relationship, anticipating the separation, and perhaps even relieved at getting away from some serious conflict and destructive action, you may be puzzled at this feeling of grief and loss. You must remember that all relationships, even bad ones, are characterized by some form of commitment and involvement. Sharing the same house, parenting the same children, planning around each other's schedules, and other interactions necessitated by living together did make your identities integrated and interdependent. The loss of this interdependence and the mutual involvement, even in a conflictual situation, causes some grief.

Sometimes the experience of grief causes both partners to assume their separation is a mistake. This may be true, but not necessarily so. A meaningful marriage must have more going for it than the experience of grief when separated.

Like many separated and divorced people you may feel that your grief would be easier to bear if your spouse had died. Death cuts with a sharp edge and leaves a deep, but clean, wound. Divorce, however, cuts with a dull edge and leaves a jagged wound which seems harder to heal. In death, the person you loved is buried; and despite some continuing fantasies the survivor knows that a continuing relationship is impossible and that real life no longer contains their spouse. In divorce, however, the person you love, or loved, is still alive. You may see them and/or talk with them regularly about children, business, money, and legal matters. You are constantly reminded that they are alive and potentially available for relationships. Both good and bad memories are continually stirred.

During separation there is no symbol, like a funeral, to symbolize the irretrievable brokenness of the relationship. Even when the final divorce is legally decreed (which can serve as a funeral of sorts), it is more difficult to move through the grief process because of the real presence of your spouse. Yet, this "working through" of the process of grief is important and needs to be accomplished if one is to claim fully an abundant life.

Many other emotions that you experience (as described below and in the chapter on depression) may be related to grief. I hope you will read chapters 7 and 8 in this book to learn more about your emotional reaction to separation and divorce. If you are anticipating separation and divorce, you might read chapter 6 on anticipatory grief.

Feelings of Failure and Loss of Self-Esteem

A major problem for people who are separated or getting a divorce is the feeling of personal failure. Our society gears us to think that success is important in any endeavor and particularly marriage. The person getting a divorce may feel a heavy burden of failure in the fact that he or she was unable to nurse the marital relationship into a mutually meaningful one. What's wrong with me? Am I so inept in personal relationships? Am I unattractive? Inadequate?

The feeling of being rejected by someone to whom you have committed yourself is a deep hurt. After being told by her husband that he did not love her anymore, one pastor's wife said:

The consuming feeling was one of total rejection, total rejection that I didn't deserve. . . . What I felt from him was, ". . . it's not what you do, it's who you are." That was the deepest hurt of all. I could not take that total rejection.

For any of us to feel worthless to another individual who knows us more deeply than any other usually produces in us a loss of personal esteem. You may have found it difficult to believe you are a lovable person. You may question whether your personality is appealing to anyone or whether anyone of the opposite sex could be attracted to you. Self-confidence and self-assurance can be threatened quickly when a marriage breaks up. One minister reported his feelings in these words:

I felt at times like a leper, a tainted person. What do I have to offer? Here [in marriage] I'm a failure. I felt like a failure. I felt guilty, because I had very high expectations of myself and there were some people who backed off from me.

You may also have strong feelings about what the divorce will do to the children. The divorced male is usually the one who leaves the children in the primary care of the mother. He may have many feelings about whether or not his absence from them will cause personality problems for the children in the future. So much literature over the last twenty years has pointed out the problems of children from "broken homes," that most people feel the existence of a broken home is certain to be a negative factor on the potential future of the children. It is important to realize that many children do much better in a separated or divorced family situation than they would if the parents stayed together, living miserable, unfulfilled, and conflictual lives just for the sake of the children. This does not change the personal emotional feelings many divorced people have about "What have I done to my children?"

Loneliness

After years of fairly constant companionship with a person with whom you went to church, attended social events, ate with, and slept with, it is difficult to suddenly be alone. You no longer have that person with whom to talk things over, to share decisions, to help with responsibilities, or to help discipline the children. You are without the regular sexual interaction, verbal exchange, and the other forms of communication which give ongoing support and security. A friend of mine, mother of three children, who had given her total self to the role of wife and mother for eighteen years, said six months after her husband left:

It is very lonely to be going back to graduate school, at age 40, not sure you can make it without any emotional support. Because there is not any one somebody who totally cares for me. . . . which may last for the rest of my life! That's a possible reality that I have to face. I don't like to think about that. I don't deal with the loneliness very well.

The acute loneliness which accompanies separation and divorce is the result of having to change from a "we" to an "I." [3] When you first got married you worked at moving from being only an "I" to being a "we." You worked at merging your life with the life of your partner. Regardless of how well the marriage worked, this was accomplished to some degree. Now you face the pain of reversing direction. You must now dissolve this merger and sever the ties which had bound you into a partnership.

You will come home at night to emptiness, eat alone, go out alone, read or watch TV alone. If you have children they keep you busy, but they only protect you from the aloneness, not the loneliness. Emptiness comes after they are in bed. Friends can be helpful, movies, parties, restaurants, and bars can all kill time, maybe even make you forget for awhile; but often they only seem like a brief diversion.

It is true that you were alone before you married and did not feel so lonely. You may ask yourself what the difference could be, perhaps underestimating how marriage changed your existence.

Marriage changes you, however. It profoundly affects your very being, whether you are aware of it or not. Your divorce cannot return you emotionally to a premarital status. You once did love; you once did have a companionship that is unlike that which you have had with your parents and unlike that which you have with your children. Having known that companionship, even imperfectly, you miss it in a way that is impossible to those who have never been married.[4]

If you wanted the divorce the loneliness might not be as intense. You may experience so much relief and freedom during the first weeks that the loneliness is not as apparent. The solitude may be welcome for awhile, the quietness refreshing, and the autonomy challenging. But sooner or later, the loneliness will be felt by you also.

It is important to deepen old relationships where possible, even though many of your married friends will not be as close. More important will be the establishment of new relationships, both with individuals and with groups, so that you can provide yourself with a community of caring people. This will be the most significant ingredient in slowly overcoming loneliness.

Guilt

You probably took your marriage seriously, and the fact that it did not work may create in you feelings of guilt. Regardless of how necessary the divorce may have been, you may still struggle with questions about your responsibility for the disintegration of the marriage. Your feelings of failure can contribute to feelings of shame and guilt.

These feelings may be complicated by all the other emotions which have been described, and as these emotions are handled the sense of guilt may diminish. However, your perception about your guilt must be taken seriously. Upon examination you may find that some of them are not valid. You may discover that you were blaming yourself for something that could not be helped or that was not your fault. On the other hand, divorce usually means that both parties contributed to the brokenness of the relationship. Some portion of your feelings of guilt, therefore, is probably valid and can be claimed by you.

As a Christian, it can be a significant expression of faith to honestly confess before God those personal shortcomings, immaturities, and irresponsibilities which contributed to the death of this relationship. God's faithfulness to forgive us of all sin should be a comfort to you. Forgiveness is a gift of God's grace and does not have to be bought or begged. You can lift your burden of guilt and shame, confess your part in the dissolution of the marriage, accept this forgiveness, and receive God's blessing.

Anger

Anger is almost always a strong ingredient in the breakup of a marriage. Although it sails under the guise of hurt, frustration, jealousy, and righteous indignation, it is usually present. You may have been angry a long time at your spouse for his or her life-style, apathy towards you, or various actions or events. Rejection causes hurt and anger. Sexual affairs illicit angry jealousy. The inability or unwillingness to communicate sparks hostile frustration.

Arguments may have been intense and heated, or perhaps your conflict manifested itself in silent wars fought from a distance. After the separation and/or divorce, the anger may be reduced for those who took the initiative and needed to get away. For those who are left and do not understand the spouse's action, anger may increase after the separation has occurred.

Finding appropriate places to handle this anger, talking with persons who can help you express it, and taking responsible action with it, is important. If the anger turns into bitterness and hate, it can become destructive to you and the children as well as interfering with the establishment of new relationships.

The Social Impact of Divorce

Separation and divorce rarely affect only one or two people. Divorce is more like the proverbial ripples that move out in ever-widening circles from the point at which a thrown stone hits the water, affecting many other people in your environment. How these others respond to your divorce can also contribute to the crisis you are going through.

Relatives

It is tougher to tell your relatives about the marital problems, separation, and/or divorce than anyone else.[5] You may have procrastinated for a long time before letting them know anything at all. Like it or not, we are usually quite attached to our family and as a result are very sensitive to the attitudes they have toward us. If you thought your family would have a negative response, you probably delayed telling them as long as possible. In fact, you may still be hiding the facts from them.

You may be one of those who has faced rejection or censure from your family or from your spouse's family. Blame may have fallen on your head. Their response may have increased your feelings of guilt and inadequacy by making you feel like the black sheep of the family.

Another problem you may be having with your parents or other relatives is their need to understand and comprehend what happened to the point where they intrude on your privacy. They ask questions you don't want to answer, yet you don't want to alienate them by refusing to share something of the emotional pain and suffering. You want to be fair to your spouse, yet not give the family the perception that you are at fault. It is difficult for them to understand "falling out of love" and they tend to look for the tangible reasons rather than the intangibles which are usually the most real.

You may have to work out the problems of autonomy again if you are back living with your parents. It is difficult for them not to treat you as if you were still their adolescent child. So they may try to give advice, be overprotective, and express judgment about your life-style.

Relatives can be very supportive, however; and if you are blessed with an understanding family who can help without intruding, listen without prying, accept without blaming, then it will be easier for you to face this crisis.

Friends

Relationships with your friends are undergoing quite a change. You cannot relate to the same community of friends (most of whom were couples) in the same way after being separated and/or divorced. Weiss's study has identified three phases through which these friendships change.[6]

At first friends rally around both partners trying to help in any way possible. They react as they would in any crisis. They offer their homes, make frequent contact, provide companionship, are willing to listen, and usually remain nonjudgmental. In the beginning weeks "couple friends" are usually friendly with both spouses, although that may change after awhile.

The second phase begins when the fact of separation becomes more permanent and friends begin to see that this crisis has a different ending. Then they begin to react in a variety of what Weiss calls "idiosyncratic reactions":

And now friends react in a wide variety of ways. Some continue to be welcoming, but others appear to feel burdened by the separated individual, as they might by anyone making too heavy a claim on their sympathies. Some seem frightened of him or her, as though the separation were a communicable disease. Some are both appalled and intrigued, as one might be with someone who had undergone a procedure so reckless as to be nearly unthinkable, like a sex-change operation. And still others react with envy, admiration, or curiosity about the separated person's assumed new freedom.[7]

Arthur Miller has cataloged many of the reactions which divorced people experience in their friends.[8] One of the most frequent responses is that of anxiety and fear. Friends whose marriage is not everything they wish it were will be threatened by the fact that your marriage came apart. They may have pictured you as an ideal couple and been unaware of your marital problems. Their emotional response is, "If it can happen to them, it can happen to me!" Some may even be ashamed that you have done something about your unhappy marriage and they have not.

Another reaction which may be disturbing to you is the sexual advances made by members of the opposite sex who have been your friends or the spouse of a friend. This happens more often to women, but also to men. This reaction grows out of the fantasies many married people have about the sexual situation and needs of divorced persons. This is often a projection of their own unfulfilled sexual drives and what they imagine themselves doing if they were unmarried.

Miller also notes that some friends will feel superior, some will be surprised and incredulous, and some will experience emotional grief over your separation.

The third phase of the change in friendship, says Weiss, is mutual withdrawal. Both you and many of your married friends will recognize that your life is different now and that the friendship is not as rewarding. The lives of married and unmarried are different. One of my divorced friends recently said: "I really am odd now. I don't fit in a lot of places I used to fit." It may not be comfortable for you to spend as much time around couples as before, even though you may maintain some friendships with the partner who is of your sex.

You will, hopefully, begin to establish a new community of people with whom to relate. They probably will be people who are also unmarried, either single, divorced, or widowed. You will also develop new friends who are married but whose spouse you do not know or seldom see, such as fellow employees or fellow club members. It is important to establish this new community.

Children

Certainly one of your major concerns is the children. How will they take it? What is the best way to tell them about it? Will coming from a "broken home" create emotional problems for them in the future?

Many couples have stayed married long past the point where divorce would have been acceptable to both, simply because they felt obligated to protect the children from the trauma of divorce and the stigma of coming from what in popular and professional terminology has come to be known as the "broken home." But you have decided that divorce is necessary despite these concerns, and some of you have decided because of these concerns.

If you are the parent with custody of the children, you may feel trapped by having to care for them as well as hold down a job. You may resent having to do the bulk of the discipline and decision-making involved in child care. You will probably experience some jealousy over the fact that the time your spouse spends with the children is usually filled with fun, economic expenditures, and gifts, while your time with them has to be so routine.

If you are the spouse without custody, your concerns will be different. You will be worried that absence from the children will slowly bring distance and separation between you and them. You may feel that they blame you for leaving or fear that your spouse will poison their minds about your part in the marriage breakup.

You may, on the other hand, feel the children are better off to be out of a situation in which they were being affected by the bitterness, anger, hostile silences, and conflict generated by the deteriorating relationship between you and your spouse. Learning to relate creatively to the children is important, but it is not always clear how to do this. Weiss has listed ten principles to help separated and divorced spouses relate to their children:

1. Children, even very young children, should be kept informed, without overwhelming them with information they cannot assimilate.
2. Children are likely to react to the separation with upset and to need appropriate solicitude.
3. Children who fail to resume normal development within a year of the separation may need special attention.
4. A competent and self-confident parent as head of the household is the child's most important source of security.
5. Preadolescent children need a parent's full attention at least part of the time.
6. Ordinarily, children gain if the noncustody parent remains in the picture.

7. It is important for the children to retain as many regions of safety in their lives as possible.

8. Insofar as there is change, children are likely to profit from parental support in establishing a satisfactory living situation for themselves.

9. Children should be permitted to mature at their own pace and neither be encouraged to become prematurely mature nor held back in their development through overprotection.

10. Parents can help their children by establishing satisfactory life situations for themselves.[9]

Conclusion

Most people still marry with the idea that their marriage will "live happily ever after." Therefore, most people are not prepared for the idea of divorce happening to them. Divorce is usually seen, like accidents, as happening to other people. This means that people in our society are not prepared for the trauma of divorce. The very fact that it is happening to you is a shocking, emotionally traumatic event.

We have described some of the major impacts of separation and divorce in this chapter. We have not, however, dealt with the religious meanings and problems raised by the issue of divorce. We will proceed to this issue in the following chapter.

Notes

1. Joseph Epstein, *Divorced in America: Marriage in an Age of Possibility* (New York: E. P. Dutton & Co., 1974), p. 11.

2. Paul Bohannan, "The Six Stations of Divorce," in Paul Bohannan, ed., *Divorce and After* (Garden City, N. Y.: Doubleday & Company, Inc., 1971), pp. 33-62.

3. Roger H. Crook, *An Open Book to the Christian Divorcee* (Nashville: Broadman Press, 1974), pp. 40-45.

4. *Ibid.*, p. 42.

5. See Robert S. Weiss, *Marital Separation* (New York: Basic Books, Inc., 1975), pp. 126-147.

6. *Ibid.*, pp. 156-162.

7. *Ibid.*, p. 158.

8. Arthur A. Miller, "Reactions of Friends to Divorce," in Paul Bohannan, ed., *Divorce and After* (Garden City, N. Y.: Doubleday & Company, 1971), pp. 63-86.

9. Weiss, pp. 226-232. Other helpful books are Earl A. Grollman, ed., *Explaining Divorce to Children* (Boston: Beacon Press, 1969) and Richard A. Gardner, *The Boys' and Girls' Book About Divorce* (New York: Science House, 1970).

10
Lord, Are You Still with Me?
(The Christian and Divorce)

The crisis of separation and divorce is complicated by the fact that social stigma is attached to this crisis but not to some of the other crises we experience. It is still true that many people are threatened by separation and divorce. Although our society moves further and further toward acceptance of divorce as a way of coping with destructive or unfulfilling marriages, there is still a strong feeling, particularly within the church, that divorce is always evil and sinful.

If you are reading this book, you are probably a Christian. If you are not a Christian, or do not have a particular religious orientation which raises concern about divorce, then you can probably divorce for humanistic and personal reasons without much regret. As a Christian, you may do the same; however, you must also deal with the fact that many other Christians think of divorce, under any circumstance, as against God's will. Some even consider it a malicious and purposeful sin, which a person could prevent if he or she wanted.

Some people will communicate to you, or you may feel of your own accord, that anyone who divorces is not a very good Christian or is not really one of the faithful. Let it be said clearly that many people are getting divorced who are Christian! Many people who are very committed to God and to his Son, Jesus Christ are deciding that to stay in their marriage is unethical and that the only way to maintain their faith and their integrity is to gain a divorce. Other good Christians would like to maintain their marriage, but their partners have decided, for whatever reasons, that they need to divorce. Neither group should feel that divorce automatically categorizes them as a non-Christian or gives them second-class Christian status.

You may have strong feelings yourself that the Bible teaches divorce under any circumstance is wrong. You may live with a feeling of guilt because of these feelings. I personally feel that to believe divorce under any circumstance is wrong is unfair to the Christian message, as we will see.

The Church and Divorce

One problem you are facing, if you are divorced or in the process of divorce, is your relationship to the church. It is difficult for some churches, and some church people, to accept divorce among Christians. Most of us have grown up hearing that divorce is a sin and knowing that most churches stand very strongly against it. Christian people have not been taught that divorce is sometimes the most ethical choice for a Christian to make. They are more often taught that the good Christian will stay in a marriage relationship regardless of its destructive nature, the harm done to both spouses and children, and the lack of fulfillment and abundant life. Therefore, many church people, even though they may like you personally, will be unsure how to relate to you as a "divorcee." Many will feel that somehow you are now a tainted or marked person. Obviously, there are others who have grown in their faith and matured to the point where they will continue to relate to you as always, understanding the trauma that you have been through, respecting your faith, and continuing to give you the supportive love that they are capable of giving.

A divorce is usually the funeral for a marriage which has died.[1] The church has had a difficult time accepting the fact that marriages do die. Christians have wanted to believe that "marriages are made in heaven," despite the fact that our personal experience and evidence accumulated over the years show that many marriages are made by mistake-prone humans who did not raise any questions about whether or not their marriage could be ordained of God. In our romantic culture, many people make terrible choices for marriage partners simply because they are not old enough, mature enough, or wise enough to know differently.

Marriage is an institution ordained by God, says the Christian church, but we must remind ourselves that this ordination does not make marriage a perfect or undefilable institution. Just as the institutional church has its failings, shortcomings, and sins, so does marriage. We must accept the fact that for some people marriage becomes a demon and not a sacrament! When a marriage dies, whatever the reasons and regardless of who has to take responsibility for its death, it is difficult for it to be resurrected. It is true, as Hudson says, that some marriages which are very sick can be resuscitated.[2] It is the goal of marriage counselors, pastoral counselors, and other therapists to help resuscitate sick marriages and to strengthen weak ones. However, since we are not God, we cannot resurrect dead relationships.

Recognizing the reality that marriages do die is important for the church. If the church is going to believe in sin and in the finitude of human beings, then it must accept the reality that relationships (some of which we call marriage) do get sick and some are terminal. When the church finally accepts this position, it can begin speaking from within the context of the Christian gospel about what to do when a marriage dies. Presently the church seems to focus its attention on pretending that marriages either do not or cannot die, rather than proclaiming to persons involved in dead or dying marriages the gospel of Jesus Christ with its emphasis on understanding, acceptance, mercy, and forgiveness.

The Bible and Divorce

Jesus spoke about divorce two different times as recorded in the New Testament. One time is recorded as part of the Sermon on the Mount (Matt. 5:31-32; Luke 16:18). The other takes place during a confrontation between Jesus and the Pharisees (Matt. 19:3-9; Mark 10:2-12). Paul also refers to Jesus' teaching on divorce (1 Cor. 7:12-16).

In the Sermon on the Mount, Jesus is commenting on a number of Old Testament laws. He seems to be reminding his hearers that

God's ideal for human relationships is deeper than we can experience if we only worry about keeping the letter of the law. We all know how easy it is to transgress the spirit of the law even while we are legalistic in following the literal law. Jesus bluntly said to these people: "For I tell you, unless your righteousness exceeds that of the scribes and Pharisees, you will never enter the kingdom of heaven" (Matt. 5:20). His specific saying about divorce points out that although divorce was legal in Judaism, it may still be sinful. What an individual can do legally is not always the most ethical thing to do. One can make choices according to the law which do not always measure up to the principles of love.

In the confrontation with the Pharisees, they ask Jesus, "Is it lawful to divorce one's wife for any cause?" (Matt. 19:3). Jesus answered by reminding them of the Genesis account of creation and the original purpose of God who created males and females who could be joined together and become one (vv. 4-6).

The Pharisees push Jesus further by asking: "Why then did Moses command one to give a certificate of divorce, and to put her away?" (v. 7). His answer was that the "hardness of heart" of human beings was the reason the law allowed divorce (v. 8). Then Jesus points out again the ideal that divorce was not in God's original plan, "but from the beginning it was not so" (v. 8).

It should be mentioned here that in Matthew's gospel there is an exception clause for divorce. In 5:32 and 19:9 it is indicated that divorce is permissible if the wife has been guilty of "unchastity." Most scholars feel this phrase was added later by the church but was not a part of Jesus' original words. Why? One reason is that this exception clause is not found in Mark's, Luke's, or Paul's reports of the same conversations. Secondly, Jesus was not legalistic, and to make one exception to God's ideal would have been "a concession to human weakness rather than a statement of what God intended for the man-woman relationship." [3]

What summary can we make of what the New Testament says about divorce? It seems clear that the Christian ideal for marriage is that it be a permanent union between a man and a woman who can give companionship, comfort, support, fulfillment, and meaning to each other's lives. To say that the ideal is any less, would be untrue to the biblical revelation.

Our problem is not in recognizing the ideal, but in dealing with the fact that as humans we fall short of this ideal. If we could all achieve perfection; be completely mature in our personalities; and know how to love God, others, and ourselves with perfect love, then there would be no need for divorce. In reality, of course, we fall way short of the ideal. As in the days of old, our human limitations, our immaturities, our "unlovingness" make it impossible for all marriage relationships to reach the ideal purposes and potentialities possible in God's creation.

Sometimes when people define divorce as a sin, they mean that anyone who gets a divorce has purposefully broken God's law. I think this definition is inappropriate, because it leaves out the moral ambiguities involved in interpersonal relationships. It leaves out the fact that in some situations divorce is the most ethical choice that a Christian can make! However, there is one way of defining sin which does allow us to understand all divorce as sinful.

Divorce does symbolize the breakdown of an interpersonal relationship, which means we have fallen short of God's ideal for our lives. When two people who have established an intimate relationship find it broken and alienated, they have "fallen short" of God's hope that we would be able to relate intimately and creatively to other humans. Obviously, this is an impossibility. When we measure ourselves against this ideal, we always come up short; and this fact is part of what the Christian faith has historically included in its concept of sin.

Christian Ethics and Divorce

So we know that the Christian ideal would be for marriages to be so loving, so fulfilling, so meaningful, that divorce would not ever be necessary. However, as in the days of Moses, when divorce was allowed because of man's imperfections, limitations, and sinfulness ("hardness of heart"), so we must recognize that marriages cannot be ethically maintained in all situations. Paul, for example, recognized that when some people become Christians their spouses would no longer wish to live with them. In that case, says Paul, the Christian should "let it be so" (1 Cor. 7:15). Here we have one example of situations in which divorce is actually the Christian thing to do.

In that same verse Paul says, "For God has called us to peace." I think Paul is saying here that marriage is meaningful and fulfilling when it is characterized by peace, which would mean a relationship characterized by happiness, joy, trust, and understanding. When the marriage is disruptive, characterized by constant fighting, mistrust, jealousy, and bitterness, then to accept the divorce is closer to God's will than to be unfulfilled or destroyed by the marriage relationship.

God did not make marriage to become an idol. To paraphrase another of Jesus' statements, God made marriage for man, not man for marriage. You had the responsibility, as a Christian, to make a judgment about whether or not your marriage was contributing to God's purpose on this earth or detracting from such purposes. If your marriage was not one in which the family members were experiencing love, joy, happiness, security, and Christian nurture, then you may consider that the decision to divorce was the most ethical choice that could be made.

It is certainly true that divorce is usually difficult and creates its own problems. However, despite the problems and negative aspects of divorce, it must be pointed out from the Christian point of view, that divorce is often necessary. By necessary, I mean that the most humane and ethical way to treat some relationships, both for the spouses' sake and for the childrens' sakes, is to end the relationship. Why? Because it has become destructive or has become so unfulfilling that it does not provide any opportunity for abundant life nor creative models for the children. In other words, in some situations divorce is the best choice and the loving thing to do. Even though divorce always means that a relationship has fallen short of its potential, divorce is sometimes an ethical choice which demonstrates mercy and justice. It therefore becomes an ethical decision and a way of following God's will. As one divorced minister shared in a seminary class:

I reasoned theologically that God values every person as an individual, and that her life as an individual and my life as an individual were more important than a bad relationship. . . . In a sense . . . the decision for us to separate was probably one of the most loving things we did for each other, because there had been so much suffering, anguish, and conflict that, as one therapist said to me, the relationship is poisonous. And that's really the way it felt.

Forgiveness and Divorce

You may decide, after careful evaluation of your marriage, that divorce in your case was the Christian thing to do. You may feel certain it was the most loving way to handle a disruptive or destructive relationship and, therefore, a wise ethical choice.

Even in this situation you may find yourself very aware that you contributed to the brokenness and estrangement that overcame the relationship. If, after careful consideration, you can identify your part in the breakup of the marriage, your contribution to it, it is appropriate to confess your share of the responsibility and to ask for God's forgiveness, as you would about any other "falling short" in your life.

Others of you will feel a much stronger sense of guilt and have doubts about whether or not the divorce was really a valid ethical decision. This will be more likely if you were the initiator in the dissolution of your marriage. You may feel yourself to be a home-breaker, to have broken God's laws, to be a failure in God's sight. You may think of yourself as a more obvious sinner than you have ever before considered. How important it is for you to be able to experience God's understanding.

You will need to resist the temptation to see divorce as some different kind of sin, one that is somehow worse than others. Some Christians will lead you to believe this is true. In some churches, divorced people are not allowed to hold offices, teach Sunday School, or participate in communion. These churches overlook the Christian proclamation about mercy and forgiveness. How important for you to remember that the God of our Lord Jesus Christ has revealed to us his willingness to forgive every human sin and every human shortcoming. God is even now loving you, caring for you, and willing to lead you toward an abundant life.

Remarriage

An important part of the crisis of separation and divorce is the decision to remarry. Two-thirds of all divorced women and three-fourths of divorced men remarry. Men usually remarry more quickly, and the younger you are the higher the chances that you will remarry. Actually, divorced persons are more likely to marry than are single persons of the same age.[4]

Remarriage has high potential for both disaster and happiness. In one study over 90 percent of the women involved in remarriages rated their second marriage as better than their first.[5] On the other hand, the divorce rate for second marriages is more than twice the divorce rate for first marriages. What can you do to increase your chances for a mutually fulfilling second marriage?

One important decision would be to take your time. So many divorcees rush too quickly into a second marriage to attempt to solve the problems of loneliness, or insecurity, or financial hardship, or sexual deprivation. They decide to get married while still angry, or grieved, or ashamed and have not "worked through" their own emotional responses to the divorce. The result is that these emotional anchors affect in a negative way their choice of a partner.

The second important factor in having a happy second marriage is the willingness to achieve a higher degree of maturity as an individual. If you were an overly-dependent wife, this might mean achieving more independence. If you were a silent and withdrawn husband, it might call for learning how to communicate with women and how to be more involved with other people.

One significant question asked by divorcees, particularly those people who are not the initiators of divorce, is, "Why?" Discussing the various reasons and causes for divorce is not one of the purposes of this chapter, but it will be important for you to learn the answer to the question "why?" Since both partners play some role, either major or minor, in the disintegration of a relationship, it can be significantly helpful to learn about the causes of the dissolution of this particular relationship. If you will take the time and expend the emotional energy to attempt to understand what has happened in your marriage, it might be of significant help to you in your other relationships and in your personal growth and development. Seeing a trained counselor might be the way for you to protect yourself against entering into other heterosexual relationships that might not be meaningful to you or to the new partner.

Many authors have pointed out how important it is for individuals to have established their own identity before entering into marriage. Of course, many of us had not achieved that level of personal insight and wisdom when we first married. In fact, one cause of divorce is when partners find their own individual identities years after the marriage began and discover that these identities do not mesh in a complementary way. As you think about a second marriage, however, you have the chance to make sure of your own identity. You will be older, more experienced, know yourself better, and can, hopefully, integrate all of those things into a more mature wisdom about yourself.

This maturity will increase your chances at successfully completing the third major factor in remarriage, making your choice of a partner a good one. Having worked through all the emotional "fall-out" from your divorce and having gained a new sense of identity will enable you to find a partner who has also "worked through" his or her major problems about a divorce or a death and established a healthy autonomy.

Because the remarks of Jesus about divorce also speak of remarriage as committing adultery (Mark 10:11-12; Matt. 5:31-32), many Christians wonder whether or not remarriage is sinful. As we have already discussed, however, Jesus is probably talking about those who use their legal rights to abuse a covenant of love. Roger Crook thinks Jesus is probably referring to those who get involved with another person and divorce their spouses simply to remarry this other person with whom they have become infatuated.[6]

Paul says, in 1 Corinthians 7:15 that the individual who is divorced "is not bound," meaning they are free from the commitments of their marriage agreement and free to marry again. It is true that in this chapter Paul seems to take a negative view toward anyone getting married. You must remember that Paul was counseling against any major change in a person's life because he thought Christ was going to return at any moment and that Christians should be concentrating on proclamation and getting ready for the kingdom of God (see vv. 20,26,29,31). He recognizes throughout the chapter, however, that marriage is either good or necessary for some and gives his okay (see vv. 2-9,28,36,38,39). Certainly Paul is not referring only to single people but to all who were unmarried.

You need to remember that God in Christ is always seeking our redemption. We are in every circumstance responsible for seeking out God's purposes for our lives. If you believe that having life more abundantly is part of God's hope for us and you feel that remarriage is one way of reaching for such abundance, then certainly God would bless your new venture into establishing the kind of oneness that is possible between males and females.

Notes

1. R. Lofton Hudson, *'Til Divorce Do Us Part* (New York: Thomas Nelson, Inc., 1973), pp. 13-25.

2. *Ibid.*, p. 18.

3. Roger H. Crook, *An Open Book to the Christian Divorcee* (Nashville: Broadman Press, 1974), pp. 40-45.

4. For statistics see Hugh Carter and Paul C. Glick, *Marriage and Divorce* (Cambridge: Harvard University Press, 1970); and William Kephart, *The Family, Society, and the Individual* (New York: Houghton Mifflin, 1972).

5. William J. Goode, *After Divorce* (Glencoe, Ill.: The Free Press, 1956).

6. Crook, p. 144.